Stephen Peg[...] [...]
of the UK's [...]
sufferers in [...]
he relied on [...]
their home i[...] [...] lived with their
young daughter Eleanor.

Stephen won the British Film Institute's
writing competition, One Day in the Life of
Television, in 1988. Two years later a film
about his life, *Just Some Stories For Eleanor*, was
made for Channel 4's Cutting Edge series, in
which he played a major role. Stephen Pegg
died in 1991.

Just
SOME STORIES
FOR ELEANOR

Stephen Pegg

CORGI BOOKS

JUST SOME STORIES FOR ELEANOR
A CORGI BOOK 0 552 13824 X

Originally published in Great Britain by Doubleday,
a division of Transworld Publishers Ltd

PRINTING HISTORY
Doubleday edition published 1991
Corgi edition published 1992

Typeset in 10.5pt Erhardt by
Falcon Typographic Art Ltd, Edinburgh

Corgi Books are published by Transworld Publishers Ltd,
61-63 Uxbridge Road, London W5 5SA, in Australia by
Transworld Publishers (Australia) Pty Ltd, 15-23 Helles Avenue,
Moorebank, NSW 2170, and in New Zealand by
Transworld Publishers (NZ) Ltd, 3 William Pickering Drive,
Albany, Auckland.

Made and printed in Great Britain by
Cox & Wyman Ltd, Reading, Berks.

For love of
Eleanor
and Ros

ACKNOWLEDGEMENTS

My brief writing career wouldn't have been possible without the love, care, advice and intervention of many people. As I'd need at least a chapter and a half to describe all the ways and times I've been cheered up, supported, encouraged or inspired, I'll restrict myself to just naming those family and friends – some old, some new – who have helped most.

Bill and Peggy Winter; Mum and Dad; Ken and Sarah Pegg; Julie and Phil, Jack and Laura Plimmer; Denise Winter; Kay Pegg; Ray and George Nikolis; Ian and Rosie Taylor; Alastair and Sheila Duncan; Linda Bell and Nicola Richards at Ham Green Hospital; Phil Armes; Marion Huang; Lans Aleeson; Eleanor Smith; all the 'dinner ladies' at Ravenswood; Reg and Sheila Jaques; Jayne Easton, Jane Mortley and Colin O'Connell at Frenchay Hospital Communication Aids Centre, Bristol; Betty and Leonard Pepperell; Ivan Rendall; Jean Thie; Bruce Dale and colleagues at St Andrew's Infants' School, Clevedon; Win Smith; Ann Morris; Margaret and Paul Hinder; Nigel and Sally Bryant; David Rees; Paul Humberstone; Carolyn, Malcolm, Gemma and Sophie Stockley; Mr Jennings; Andy and Marion Hunt; Elaine Withey; James Edwards; John Richardson; Andy Brice (Medical Physics Department) and the nurses of Ward J, Southmead Hospital; Margot Dalzell; Hal; Glyn Vaughan; Philip Yates; Kathy and Steve Hampton; David Green; Janet Willis; Beryl Griffiths; Martin Bartley; John Pugh; Margaret Pilbeam; Pat and Rob Burn; Jeff Stoneman; Roland Clark; Andrew Bullock; Bob and Diz Smithbone; Vee Hawkins and the Clevedon District Nurses; Sarah Bayliss; Anna Massey; Karen Royce and Dave Greensill; Billy Blake; Eleanor and Ros Pegg.

27 December 1990

Contents

FOREWORD

The first sight of Stephen Pegg can be quite shocking. His wife, Ros, wheels him into the room. You notice the hands and legs first. They stick straight out in front, quivering spasmodically, the fingers bent back unnaturally. The head lolls forward onto the chest; only the eyes move in your direction. With considerable skill and effort Ros pulls him towards her, up onto her shoulders, then manoeuvres him round and onto the bed, lifting his legs into position. Only now does he turn his head a fraction and smile. He sees, hears, feels and thinks but he cannot move and he cannot speak.

I first met Steve while researching a commission to make a film on Motor Neurone Disease. In retrospect I'm unsure of my enthusiasm for the project at that time, being reluctant to make another of those films about someone dying bravely. We talked at first, in the way you do in the Pegg household, where questions to Steve are skilfully, often intuitively answered by Ros. I knew Steve had won a national diary-writing competition; I didn't know he had written anything else. Ros fetched a pile of manuscript, all written since the onset of his illness, and deposited it in my lap. I remember how oddly unnerving it was to sit at the bedside reading those pieces, which were witty and clever, sometimes cynical, occasionally sad, usually funny, always well-written – and then to look up at the rag-doll figure of their author on the bed staring (seemingly) emptily at the television screen. With Stephen Pegg, I had to tell myself, what you see is not what you get.

So out went the film about a disease and in came a film written by and starring Stephen Pegg. An actor spoke his words. We called it *Just Some Stories for Eleanor* from a line in the opening dedication. But if there was an omission in the film, then it was of the 'stories' themselves, whose narrative could not be encompassed in a documentary. Ironically, in that same dedication, he also wrote: 'These stories, letters, poems – whatever ultimately ends up gathered together by your mum – are not intended for commercial publication . . .' It has taken extraordinary and cruel circumstances for Steve's talent to flourish and to achieve recognition. I can think of no more deserved a reward than to see his work finally published as literature in its own right.

IAN TAYLOR
January 1991

POSTSCRIPT TO THE PAPERBACK EDITION

Steve received his first copy of *Just Some Stories for Eleanor* in April 1991, a month before the date of publication. The publishers had sent the book, at Ros's request, by special courier. Steve's mother and brother came for the weekend. The family turned the pages for him and read excerpts aloud. Eleanor made a banner which read I LOVE DADDY and everyone sang 'For he's a jolly good fellow'. Four days later, on 24 April, he died.

WELL, A LONG TIME AGO . . .

I was half-awake in a hospital bed in Bristol when Brian Redhead told me that John Lennon was dead. I was recovering after a small exploratory operation which had been hastily arranged when it was feared I might have Hodgkin's Disease. After a few tears and a fortnight of unspoken fears a consultant told me that I didn't have cancer. Imagine each day's Christmas, it's easy if you try.

Life is very short, and there's no time, for fussing and fighting, my friend. So I resolved to make the most of my reprieve, filling the next six and a half years with holidays, meals out, sport in the evenings and at weekends. It was while playing squash that I first sensed a weakness in my right hand and arm. I began losing more games than I was winning. I assumed I had a sports injury and rested, but it didn't make any difference. Tests followed and in May 1987 I was informed that I had Motor Neurone Disease. Although I attempted to minimize the devastation by recalling my earlier good fortune, observing a death sentence pronounced upon a man you know is strangely surreal. Such things only happen to someone else – a character in a novel, an actor in a play, an unknown person in a television documentary. I always hoped I'd never be the local paper's tragedy-of-the-week, the ghost of a recent photo staring at all my neighbours above an ill-written human interest half-column. Yet there I was, and here I am, the reluctant story in search of a happy ending.

It's hard to describe the overwhelming sadness I felt after taking Eleanor swimming for the final time because I was no longer able to dress myself. Even more painful was realizing that I'd never again be able to read her a story, as my croaky voice ran out of expression on a dual carriageway near Exeter. We were returning from Cornwall, having spent our last family holiday together.

Being told I had an incurable illness did, surprisingly, have at least one redeeming feature. Very few of us choose the time and manner of our going; we're here one morning and then are suddenly gone before we can shout goodbye. Having had advance notice of my departure I've tried to use what's left of my life to say goodbye in the only way I can. Unable to get out and do, I now stay in and write.

I started writing an occasional diary and the odd introspective poem in December 1987, six months after MND-Day. In November 1988 I submitted an entry for the British Film Institute's 'One Day in the Life of Television' diary-writing competition. In April 1989 I heard that my diary had been selected as the best of 18,000 entries, and shortly afterwards my winning piece appeared in the *Guardian*. When the newspaper sent me a cheque a few weeks later I was instantly transformed from escaped teacher to full-time writer.

When I was a teacher I'd regularly written for a small and unappreciative audience of children and their parents. My reports were never short-listed for the 'Baker Prize'. Now I write for my own child. She laughs at my silly verse. She is enormously proud whenever I have something published. She tells her friends I'm famous.

I've written about my love for my daughter, Eleanor, a love I feel more acutely than most fathers since I can no longer do with her the things that an able-bodied, loving dad would. I've also written about my childhood and schooldays, the sort of tales I would have told her as she grew up. I hope that my stories will amuse and entertain her and my wife when I'm no longer around.

My success in the BFI competition brought me to the attention of Ian Taylor, an independent film director who was researching for a film about Motor Neurone Disease. The eventual outcome of his first visit in July 1989 was that some of my writing featured in his film, *Just Some Stories for Eleanor*, which was shown on Channel Four.

Why would a man who always hoped he'd never be featured as tragedy-of-the-week in the *Clevedon Mercury* allow four strangers into his home to film his frailty, focus on his wasted limbs and record his distorted speech? Well, my daughter thinks I'm famous so I thought I'd better flirt with celebrity and claim my fifteen minutes of fame. Fifteen turned to fifty, though. That's inflation for you.

Film-making is not the glamorous life that it's made out to be. It's tiring, tedious, repetitive, slow. Film-makers are good company, though. We enjoyed having the crew around, despite the extra work their presence created. I think they must have been workhouse boys together in an earlier existence, always wanting 'more' of something or other. Ian kept asking me to write more words to go with the latest filmed sequence; Tom, the cameraman, forever wanted 'more cable'; Stan the sound man lived in the cake tin, emptied it regularly, requested more fruit loaf and chocolate sponge; Martin, the focus puller, cable carrier, camera loader, light lugger, gate checker and clapperboard chalker, didn't say much but I suspect he wanted more hands and more time. Don't we all?

MND-Day changed the direction of my life in ways both bad and good. If I'd never been ill I wouldn't be haltered here between two micro switches and staring at a computer screen, deadlines dangling noose-like above my ego. Instead, I might have been running up and down a football pitch, queuing in Safeway, washing the car or gardening. I imagine I might have been doing something with Eleanor – mending her bike, perhaps, or taking her to a pantomime, or browsing through my record collection.

'Who's that funny-looking man, Dad?'

'John Lennon, Ellie.'

'Does he still make music?'

'Not any more.'

'Why not?'

'Well, a long time ago, when you were just a story in my head, I was half-awake in a hospital bed in Bristol when . . .'

NORTHERN SONGS,
SOUTHERN VOICE

1

How many more like me, anchored alone?
A few grown slowly older with young McCartney,
others left or leaving early, just like John,
all of us living out our lives through the words
of some half-remembered Northern songs?

2

Day after day, I'm alone in my room
and pointing at gardens in my past,
getting back to places where I used to run.
Once a man who saw himself a winner
but knew it couldn't last,
I raced against impending misfortune,
feet in clay, arms waving on play,
my head forever a fool in the clouds.

3

He eventually returned to His consulting room –
such a tiny room for the enormity of His task –
nervously licked His lips with silver tongue,
swallowed, sighed, looked between my eyes, began.

He claimed that He would get no pleasure
but tapped His mallet on my knee,
and then when I least suspected
said He couldn't help,
stole up to rob me of all hope.

'Help you, if I could. Don't feel down.
I do appreciate you hanging around
for the news I have to tell.
MOTOR – NEURONE – DISEASE
These are words which go together well.'

He said he'd always been in neurones,
worked for fifteen hours each day,
and though He always knew the answers
He never quite knew what to say.

Consulting His thumb with silver tongue,
suddenly all those fifteen hours were repaid
as inspiration told Him to smile and hand me
His remaindered paperback copy
of the *Which Good Hospice Guide*.
People say He was only fooling,
but I know He really wasn't.

I heard the news today – it's bad.
Another unlucky man woke up, lost in bed,
four thousand holes where his neurones used to be.
And though the holes were rather small
the latest scanner showed them all,
computed in microseconds, a print-out in colour,
available in English, Spanish and Japanese.
Now they know how many holes
it takes to make my disease.

4

Help! We need somebody, something,
to fill our days with sunshine.
Some day, same day, yesterday.
Yesterday, all my troubles seemed
like the echo of an old tabloid cliché.

I was alone at home and looking for a cure
when I found an invitation to join *Guardian* readers for

an Austrian medical mystery tour.
At Lourdes-am-Tirol we queued with the ill, incurables,
walking wounded, men and women on their last wheels.

Doctor Marx made blue sparks leap from his
   fingertips
for twenty-five pounds and filled my head with hope,
gave me strength to walk a corridor and talk till
   midnight.
I dreamed of leaving broken wings,
forever singing good day songs,
but I'm still here.
Feels like years since I've been here.

5

Writing a sermon for a man I used to know,
I'm waiting for a visit from another John.
Will he bring me a pudding, made from the rice
he picked from his path where a wedding has been,
or a headful of stories told by the ladies
of 'The Lonely People (Registered) Rest Home'?

6

Standing alone at the top of the stairs,
my daughter clutching books I bought
long before she was a twinkling in my eye,
books I cannot read to her,
send her dreaming, sleep little darling.
Hush little darling, don't you cry,
I never had the voice for lullabies.

7

No-one sang in the ear of my friend Bernard,
   life is very short.

Ten years after we fell
from his bike on an Eastcote hill,
grazed our knees and elbows and tore a hole
in his long trousers, ten years after we fell
Bernard fell again. Far away
from rugby fields, one more unlucky man
touched down, somewhere in Vietnam.
Eight lines and his photograph in the *Ruislip Post*,
reluctant conscript to Lennon's ghosts.

8

Nobody warned Leontes after his last school play.
It all seems like strawberry fields to me,
nothing real and everything ordered wrong,
but his mother wrote me a long letter,
her only son in a sad song
and no-one there to make the final scene better,
better better better better.

I'm waiting in the wings for black-out and scene change
when the bear rushes in – very strange.
Penny Lane is also in this play,
her Triumph Herald, hair silver grey,
soon takes charge of the situation,
attacks the beast with revised edition.
There beneath the blue Bohemian skies
she demonstrates the difference
between infers and implies,
pursues bear downstage, down steps and
out into the crowded hall.
After so many years of suspended disbelief
do they see the bear at all?
They gasp, they laugh, they listen,
queue for coffee and biscuits,
swop old news for new gossip,
yet how many notice Leontes missing?

Do you need anybody?
Yes, I need someone to wash me, dress me, feed me,
scratch my back, pick my nose,
stretch my fingers, move my arms and legs.

Could it be anybody?
No, I need someone I love, someone I trust;
someone who looks at me when I try to talk;
someone who doesn't ask me how I feel,
how am I doing, all right?

Does it worry you to be alone?
No, I've always been a part-time loner,
sometimes a stranger to my own shadow.
My love's grown quiet, that worries me.

What do you see when you look in her eyes?
I can't tell you, but it used to be mine.

When she's sixty-four I hope she's happy,
I hope she's healthy – stuff the wealthy –
another Eleanor's sparkle in her eyes.

I'll not grow older slowly, lose my hair,
view the world through eyes grown dimmer,
do my garden, hoe the weeds,
edge the lawn, prune the apple trees,
get by with a little help from
my Health Service Leaseplan zimmer.

I'm leaving notes, letters, poems,
all my football programmes,

all my Beatles magazines,
all my love in just some stories.
I would like to have left more
but I ran out of time,
had to keep an appointment I'd made.
Someone tell her, baby your daddy's gone,
left home early, hand in hand with John.
He's sleeping now in some other giant's garden,
sleeping like a log.

TEA ON SUNDAYS

Before I left my primary school for the sophistication of grammar school in posh, middle-class Ickenham, I was a simple soul from a council estate. Life consisted of schooldays and holidays, weekdays and weekends, visits and being visited. Most visits took place on Sundays, that being the one rare day when my dad might be at home. Our most frequent visits were made to grandmothers, especially when they both lived in nearby Acton. Not surprisingly, Nana Foster and Nana Pegg were also our most frequent visitors.

When I was very young I simplistically divided all my relatives into Fosters and Peggs, although I knew that there were also Pyes, Robinsons and Hedges. I also ordered the families according to status, income and occupation, but not through snobbery. I was the sort of boy who liked to collect and catalogue all kinds of things, and family information was just another category with which to play. The Ruislip Gardens Peggs were, I reckoned, near the bottom of the income league – but only because we were the largest family. I suppose I regarded the two insurance-agent uncles, Bob Hedges and George Pye, as top of the status pile since they were buying their homes and owned the largest cars. Dad, working in the theatre, appeared to have the most-envied occupation, closely followed by Aunty Rene Hedges who was a telephonist/receptionist at Twickenham Film Studios.

Mum's brother Jack and his wife Peggy emigrated to Australia in about 1955, so we could only dream of them visiting us or, better still, us visiting them. Her other brother, Uncle Ernie, lived in Fulham with Aunty

Rene, cousins Carol and Barry and no car. The transport problem was Uncle Ernie's excuse for rarely visiting, but I suspect that his love of a Sunday lunchtime booze-up at the Greyhound was the real reason.

We didn't see much of our other Aunty Rene either. I always sensed friction between her husband, Uncle Bob, and my parents, although nothing was ever said. We used to see their daughter, Sally, quite often, though, when the cousins got together at Nana Pegg's house in Southend. The other insurance agent in the family, Uncle George, visited even less frequently than Uncle Bob. They probably offered the same excuse – 'Bookwork'. Dad's brother, Uncle Bill, was another without a car so we went to his Langley home if we wanted to see cousins, Bill, John and Sheila, and Aunty Phyl.

The most frequent visitors were Eve and Bert Robinson and our cousins Chris and Barbara. Aunty Eve was a tailoress, a very talented one, who made me many an overcoat, pair of trousers or suedette slipover. Whenever she visited, one or more of us Pegg children would have to endure a fitting or pinning or measuring session before we were allowed out to play. In addition to making clothes for family and neighbours, Eve taught dressmaking several nights a week at a Further Education college somewhere near her Stoke Newington home. Uncle Bert was head park keeper in a large LCC park not far from the River Lea, and always wore his park keeper's suit and boots when he visited. This was a regular source of family fun, as was Uncle Bert's deafness.

'He's only deaf when he chooses,' Aunty Eve used to say. 'Deaf when I want him to do something, but he always hears when his supper's on the table.'

We occasionally travelled in Dad's three-wheeled Bond Minicar to see the Robinsons, but they seemed eager to escape from bleak north London to the leafy suburbs so more often came to us. At first they travelled by bus and Underground – Aunty Eve being made of sterner stuff than certain car-less uncles. When she later bought herself a Ford Anglia, Eve and the Robinson family became even more frequent visitors to Stafford Road.

There were certain rituals associated with tea on Sundays, most of them exceedingly mundane and guaranteed to make us children more fractious than normal, but Aunty Eve could add incident and hilarity to the most ordinary of Sundays. The first ritual – the one that I most abhorred – was Aunty Eve's greeting kiss. Eve was a very striking, attractive woman but, in the style of the times, was so heavily powdered and thickly lipsticked that after even the briefest embrace I smelt like the perfume counter in a chain store and had a greasy red smudge somewhere on my face. To make matters worse, if Eve saw the evidence of her affection she'd open her black patent handbag, produce a clean white handkerchief, unfold it, indiscreetly moisten a corner with saliva and proceed publicly to wipe me clean. Nowadays, being so disabled, I rely on Ros to make me presentable. If she ever attempts to do a quick repair job with spit and tissue I instantly recoil from the scented face of Aunty Eve, hovering above me and poised to strike.

The second ritual that I readily recall was the table laid for tea with best china and cutlery. These were not, as you might imagine, prized Coalport and Georgian silver inherited from a wealthy spinster aunt who had been given them by one of Queen Victoria's physicians. These were cups, saucers and plates which had somehow survived the clumsy fingers of Julie and me, plus the shiniest and straightest spoons, knives and forks which hadn't been swapped by Mike for a go on Billy Fox's racing bike. Needless to say, the least chipped crockery and least bent cutlery was placed in front of our visitors.

We usually ate salad – tinned pink salmon salad – with plates of thinly-sliced, sparingly-buttered bread, a David Greig Victoria sponge and Cadbury's chocolate fingers.

Before our visitors had arrived we'd been warned by Mum, 'That's all there is so don't ask for any more!' Unaccustomed to such a delicacy, most of the children declined the tinned salmon, anyway, and made ourselves salad sandwiches. If Chris or Barbara took the last chocolate finger Julie and I would exchange conspiratorial glances, determined to have our revenge the next time we were in Stoke Newington for Sunday tea.

The choice of rich tinned salmon wasn't the only adult ploy aimed at reducing our overall food consumption. Aunty Eve would have already done her bit on arrival at the house. As soon as the kissing had been dispensed with she would hand us children an enormous bag of boiled sweets – occasionally there were toffees for a change – accompanied by a warning not to 'eat them all before tea'. Some chance! I suppose it's rather cynical to suspect the adults of plotting to suppress our appetites when it is obvious how much we were loved. Better to explain the disregard for our dental well-being as a backlash to the sweet rationing that had not long since ceased. Even today, people of our parents' generation are great confectionery and biscuit consumers. Observe them in a theatre, tea shoppe or in front of the television and you'll see what I mean.

The passing of time has, no doubt, coloured my view of Sunday teatime rituals, and I may have embellished the occasional anecdote here and there. However, there's one constant element to tea with the Robinsons that has no need of hyperbole or artistic licence. Whatever the weather, whatever games the children were in the middle of playing, however busy the roads might be, however sick Barbara was feeling from eating too many boiled sweets and the last chocolate finger, as soon as Aunty Eve had drained the last drop of PG from her cup she would thank my mum, ask for her family's coats and declare her intention to leave promptly. She never once offered to help clear the table or wash up.

Although we came to expect this rapid departure – indeed we wouldn't have known how to respond if Eve had offered a hand – it always annoyed Mum. After we'd waved them away she would survey the tea table – here a crumb, there a crust, an empty salad-cream bottle, a hoard of teaspoons where my brother had been sitting – and remark with a mixture of laughter and despair, 'Well, she's done it again. Your sister's done it again.' And she'd look at Dad, vainly hoping that he might offer an apology or an explanation for his sister's behaviour. Julie probably said, 'Never mind, Mum. I'll wash up. Go and have a sit-down in the front room.' I probably picked up a Sunday paper and sneaked out to the toilet to study the football results. Mike probably stuffed something in his trouser pocket and went over the road to see if Billy Fox and his track bike were in.

Whenever the Robinsons came over on a Sunday afternoon I would stop fighting with Mike, Julie would stop squabbling with me, and we'd all three agree an unseen and unspoken temporary peace treaty in the interest of family solidarity. Julie and Barbara usually got on well together, occasionally arguing over something trivial, whereas Chris and I often fought. Despite the best efforts of our respective parents to bribe us with sweets or distract us with games, Chris and I soon progressed from play to competition, through argument and threats to a wrestling contest which inevitably ended in defeat for me. I knew that I was destined to lose, Chris being older, stronger and a better fighter than me, but he always employed the infuriating tactic of allowing me to win the opening exchanges. He'd pretend he was scared as I sat on his chest and demanded that he 'Submit! Submit!' but I rarely managed to pin his shoulders to the floor beyond a count of 'One, two, three . . .' before I was dumped unceremoniously in a heap, Chris climbing astride me and loudly counting to ten.

Although our fights always followed the same predictable pattern I still got upset, my pride steamrollered time and again by Chris. His mum would survey us, allow herself a moment of maternal triumph, and then announce, 'That's enough, Chrissie, off you get.' At the same time she'd be unclipping the catch on her black patent handbag and preparing to add insult to injury by wiping at my tears with her chloroforming hankie. My mum, grasping an opportunity to contribute something profound while Eve heaved her huge bosom and drew breath, would say, 'It always ends in tears. It was the same last time.' Uncle Bert would just sit there saying nothing and smiling benignly, his distorted and inverted image reflected down at me from the silver case of his park-keeper's fob watch. Dad, frantically trying to retrieve my name from the jumbled filing cabinet inside his head, would come up with, 'Stop that crying, Michael. Act your age.' I was eleven, my brother seven. The final humiliation. Everyone, including Bert, laughed. I crawled and bawled behind the settee.

On another Sunday afternoon, one summer before my eleventh birthday, I was involved in another fight, but this time Chris was not my opponent, nobody laughed at my expense and Aunty Eve was in my corner. On this particular Sunday my opponent was the reigning Home Counties Biteweight champion, Steven Ash.

The Ash family lived opposite us, between the Church family and the Pughs. Steven was the third of four brothers, and went through junior school in the same class as Julie; Kenneth was a couple of years older than me; Robert was in my class, and one of my best friends; Graham was only a baby. Mr Ash was an unusual resident of Ruislip Gardens, being a member of the managerial class. He supervised the manufacture and installation of church organs at a small factory in Bridgewater Road, just on the South Ruislip side of the Central Line.

Other fathers of my friends were employed in a variety

28

of jobs, mostly clerical or semi-skilled, but few of them aspired to managerial status. Mr Taylor was a carpenter; Mr Church had an office job with British Railways; Mr Lucas drove London buses; Mr Clegg and Mr Pugh worked at London Airport; Mr Fox was a coalman; Mr Draper, curiously enough, was a draper; Mr Beasley was an insurance agent; Mr James supervised a United Dairies depot; Mr Bush delivered cakes for Lyon's at Greenford.

I cannot recall any of these men ever being unemployed during the fifties but Mr Ash, ironically, was the first to be made redundant when his factory closed in the mid-sixties. Unsurprisingly, though, he became the first self-employed resident when he bought himself a share of West End Cycles in New Pond Parade and helped run the shop with Mrs Ash and their sons.

Mrs Ash had become an entrepreneur a number of years earlier, long before enterprise, self-employment and small businesses became fashionable. She bought herself a pair of electric clippers, converted an old cotton sheet, balanced a small stool on a table in her kitchen and began to trim the locks of local boys for sixpence a visit. I never much liked having a haircut, but I preferred the short walk over the road to Mrs Ash for a brief but gentle tidying-up of my Adam Faith hairstyle to the long journey to the hairdressers in West End Road. There I would have to wait for ages amidst the cigarette smoke and brilliantine, Brylcreem and piles of old movie magazines before being sat on a board which rested precariously across the slippery arms of a barber's chair. Then I would be roughly handled by someone called Tony or André, my ears snipped, the mole on my head half-severed and sufficient trimmings to stuff a three-piece suite deposited down the back of my shirt. Mrs Ash was quicker, kinder, cheaper, and she didn't expect a tip.

If I walked across Stafford Road and found another

little boy perched atop the tower in Mrs Ash's kitchen, I would wait in the garden and watch Mr Ash's budgerigars. There were dozens, housed in a cage almost as big as Julie's bedroom. It was while waiting for my haircut that Kenneth Ash, reckoned to be the most sensible Ash boy since he had won a scholarship place at St Clement Danes, speared me in the ankle with a dart. He claimed it was an accident but his mum and I knew better. Mrs Ash, alerted by my budgie-deafening cries of pain, rushed from her kitchen, gently eased the dart from my ankle, cleaned the wound, admonished her son, gave me a drink of home-made ginger beer and cut my hair for free. I kept quiet about the incident and later spent the sixpence on chips.

Mr and Mrs Ash were unusual in other ways. They were, as far as I knew, the only council house tenants in the world who employed a cleaner, but I suppose that their many commercial activities made household staff essential. Later they became one of the first families to buy their council house under the right-to-buy scheme, the first to fit replacement aluminium windows and the first to have their house clad with those pastel-toned mock concrete Lego bricks which are so favoured by some right-to-buy schemers. The Ash family was also one of the first to own a new car, as distinct from a used car; the first to have a separate car for the wife; and the first with a large estate car. I don't list some of their employment, housing and automotive firsts through envy since I think they deserved the rewards that their hard work earned. I only want to illustrate how different the Ash family was.

None was more different than Kenneth Ash. The incident with the errant dart fairly reflects his attitude towards me – he didn't like me. This was very probably because I usually had too much to say for myself. Instead of biting my tongue when I heard or witnessed something contentious, I would happily make my own contribution to any argument. Often, I'll say in my own defence, I would witness the misfortunes of some other boy and go to his aid. Whatever the reason, I frequently ended up with a split lip or bloody nose at the bottom of some gang's 'Bundle!' or was pushed backwards over a wall into someone's hedge.

I don't wish to give the impression that I was forever fighting, or in tears as a result of fighting, but there were gangs and rivalries. The most powerful gangs and individuals were those that threatened most loudly and fought most often, but the fighting was never life-threatening and was always conducted within a code of unwritten but mostly well-observed rules. Those I remember were:

1. No gouging, biting, throwing stones or use of sticks.
2. Kicking of legs permitted, but not kicking of heads.
3. Scratching by boys distinctly frowned upon and to be discouraged. Scratching in girls' fights tolerated and, anyway, what do you expect?
4. Spitting illegal.
5. All fights to end when one party says 'Give in' (sob), in response to question 'Give in?' (snarl).

Most rules were obeyed by most boys most of the time, but all rules were regularly broken by Steven Ash all of the time. He was especially fond of scratching and biting. I really can't remember the cause of our Big Fight but it was almost certainly trivial. Events probably unfolded like this.

A sunny Sunday afternoon. Julie Pegg, Carole Pugh, Irene Lucas and Barbara Robinson are skipping on the pavement outside the Pughs' house. Stephen Pegg, Robert Ash and Chris Robinson are playing football in the road, using the school entrance gates as a goal and Robert as a reluctant goalkeeper. Mike Pegg, Billy Fox and Steven Ash are playing marbles in the gutter outside the school. Kenneth Ash is doing nothing in particular, just lurking, occasionally dropping gravel down a drain.

31

Barbara trips over while skipping, falls awkwardly and immediately begins to cry loudly.

Steven Ash laughs.

I say, 'What are you laughing at, Ash?'

Kenneth Ash says, 'Nothing, Pegg.'

'Not you,' I quickly make clear. 'Him,' I add, pointing at the hyena sitting on the kerb.

'Come here and say that again, Pegg,' Kenneth threatens.

'Want to change?' I ask Robert Ash, hoping to divide and fool.

'I'll go in goal.'

Steven Ash continues laughing. Chris and Julie escort a hobbling Barbara back to our house. Kenneth Ash's eyes narrow and he menacingly moves gravel into a pile in the gutter with the toes of his shoes. I gently roll my Frido ball in Robert Ash's direction. His first shot trickles under my outstretched right leg, probably because I am watching his lurking elder brother out of both corners of both eyes. Kenneth Ash tires of stockpiling gravel and goes home to terrorize budgerigars.

Mike, taking advantage of Steven Ash's laughing fit, sneaks six silver bullbies (ball bearings) from Steven's marbles bag and slips them into his own trouser pocket.

Billy Fox elbows Steven Ash in the ribs and enquires, 'You playing or what?'

Steven Ash's automatic response is to pick up his marbles bag and swing it in the direction of Billy Fox's head. As he does so the finely-calibrated Ash register inside his brain activates an alarm. He knows his bag is lighter, and he knows exactly what is missing.

'Six bloody bullbies!' he bellows, switching target and attempting to decapitate my brother.

Mike flees with Billy Fox to the sanctuary of Billy's front garden where Larry Fox, fifteen and a teddy boy, nonchalantly plays with a garden fork.

I observe all this from my goalmouth, check that

Kenneth Ash hasn't ceased budgie-baiting and, encouraged by his continued absence, laugh at Steven Ash.

Steven swears at me.

I ensure that Kenneth the Menace hasn't returned from force-feeding gravel to his father's budgies before sneering at Steven Ash and daring him to 'Come here and say that again.'

He does.

I push him in the stomach with plastic football.

He attempts to kneecap me with flailing marbles bag.

Fight of the Fifties commences in earnest, in road, in front of small crowd.

Once again my ill-controlled tongue had got me into a tricky situation. Being the younger combatant, Steven Ash probably had the support of the uncommitted neutrals in the crowd, like Mike. I couldn't inflict a crushing defeat on him for fear of being labelled a bully, but I couldn't run away for fear of losing face. If I prolonged the fight to engineer an honourable draw Kenneth Ash would probably turn up and throw me through the Jacksons' hedge, so my only choice was to battle it out.

I was never much good at fighting. My record at that time was something like: Fought 97, Won 27, Drawn 34, Lost 36. Most of my wins were over Mike, nearly all my defeats inflicted by Chris Robinson, and almost every drawn scrap was a brief playground encounter in which both contestants refused to 'Give in' (sob), and retired to fight another day.

Steven Ash was, without doubt, the most tigerish of all the Ruislip Gardens fighters. His brother Kenneth may have been the most sadistic, Alec McDermott may have been the toughest and Dick French the most feared, but none of them possessed Steven Ash's deadly claws and tiger's teeth. He was pretty deadly with a marbles bag, too.

I had to wrestle that marbles bag from him before he smashed me over the head or between the legs, thereby

33

ruining my chances either of passing the eleven plus or of becoming a father. However, as I attempted to disarm him he attempted to dishand me, biting me just below the thumb. Bashing me hard on the right ear with his own marbles bag made him release his fangs momentarily, but they were soon attached to another part of my right arm. This time I nearly had to strangle him before he stopped biting, but he only stopped long enough for a snarl to emanate from his throat before his canine teeth gripped my left leg just below the hem of a torn trouser leg and above a grazed knee.

'You bloody bastard. Fight properly,' I shouted, but he just bit harder. I struggled more wildly, shouted out more loudly. Steven unclamped his teeth once more, pointed his fingernails towards my face, took a deep breath and lunged at my neck with mouth open and a full set of gnashers displayed fearsomely.

This mismatch went on for some time, time enough for me to be bitten on hands, arms, legs and neck, and scratched on cheeks and ears; time enough for me to begin to bite him back; and time enough for Kenneth Ash and my cousin Chris to come out and separate us.

Chris took me home, exchanging threats and aggressive postures with Kenneth Ash. Aunty Eve and my dad stood by the front door.

'Look what that Ash boy's done, Mum,' said Chris, one arm placed protectively around my shoulder and the other pointing at bite marks.

'No, Chrissie, no! Is that right, Steve?' asked an incredulous Aunty Eve, taking me into the front room and shouting towards the kitchen where Mum and Julie were making a start on the Sunday tea.

'Come here, Peg. Look at this. Stop that, Peg, and look at this. That can wait. Just you see this.'

Well, my mum had seen it all before, on many occasions. Never quite as bad as this, it's true, but she knew what Steven Ash could do. Aunty Eve couldn't believe Mum's complacency.

'Now look here, Peg, this isn't right. It's tough where we live, isn't it Chrissie? But the kids round our way fight fair, don't they Bert? Bert! Isn't that right, Bert?'

Uncle Bert looked up from the City page of his *Sunday Express* and concurred with a smile and a gentle nod.

There must have been at least half a dozen bite marks on my body, blue and red evidence revealing that Steven Ash possessed a full set of teeth.

'Get some Dettol, Peg. Get those bites cleaned,' ordered Aunty Eve. 'Now, where does that little biter live?' she asked, smoothing her skirt and checking that her stocking seams were straight.

'Don't go over there,' Mum pleaded. 'Don't make a fuss.' Aunty Eve bristled. 'A fuss, Peg. What do you mean? I'm sorry, Peg, but we can't let him get away with that sort of thing.' Without waiting for counter-arguments she bustled out of our house, Chris beside her as navigator.

We all watched from behind the net curtains in the front room, shushing Mum quiet so that we might hear some of the confrontation between Aunty Eve and Mrs Ash. Steven Ash was cowering behind his mother in the front doorway while both women took turns to point at him. Aunty Eve's arm movements resembled bayonet thrusts, whereas Mrs Ash gently gestured towards her son in the manner of Jesus on a Sunday School attendance stamp. We couldn't make out any particular words above Aunty Eve's nonstop bandsaw tirade, so I imagined Mrs Ash trying to counter with a Sunday School quote.

'John 7, verse 24. "Judge not according to the appearance." Your nephew may have bite marks but look at my son. He's all upset.'

Mrs Ash made the mistake of bringing Steven out from behind her skirt to show just how all upset he was. At this moment Aunty Eve lunged at Steven Ash, grabbed his arm and bit him. This was so unexpected that everyone, the Ash family at 46 Stafford Road and the spectators at 65, gasped and stood open-mouthed. This gave Aunty Eve the opportunity to retreat before Mrs Ash had time to react. When she went to follow my aunt, Mr Ash restrained his angry wife, obviously aware that she was no match for the Stoke Newington Amazon.

Aunty Eve came into our front room triumphantly, her bosom puffed out with pride, a broad grin painted across her face in her favourite red lipstick.

'He won't bite your Steve again, Harold,' she declared. 'A bit of his own medicine, he understands that all right, Peg. He won't bite anyone again in a hurry, will he, Bert?'

Uncle Bert, having been completely unaware of the drama enacted only thirty yards from his City page, looked at his better half, stood up and said, 'Yes, please. I hope Peg's done one of her salmon salads.'

My dad often worked on Sundays, from the time he was at 'Q' Theatre until his retirement from the Piccadilly Theatre in 1986. While he was away the children did play. Play up their mother, mostly.

'Just wait until your father gets back,' she'd threaten. Quite often, before Dad got back, an accident occurred. There were the usual fingers trapped in doors, broken window panes, grazed knees and hits on the head with a cricket bat. There were also less frequent happenings, like an arm stuck fast between the railings of a fence, setting fire to long grass with stolen matches, dropping house keys down a drainhole. And then there were the dramatic ring-for-an-ambulance incidents, invariably involving Mike and me, Mike in trouble and me in the ambulance.

The first of these happened when I was about eight and Mike five. Our back garden was approximately seventy yards long and divided into two sections by Dad's small workshop, 'The Shed', and a rose-covered trellis.

A concrete path ran down the left side of the garden, from our back door to the trellis. Flowers were grown in the borders and near to the house. Just to the left of the start of the path was Mum's rockery, her pride and joy, topped by a gunmetal statuette of Hercules. Just above the rockery was a lime tree, and beyond that two small apple trees. In the second section of garden was the stage caravan from 'Q', the vegetable patch and the compost heap.

Between the two sections, next to The Shed and almost hidden by the trellis, was a metal water butt which collected rainwater from The Shed roof. When Dad first installed the butt he sometimes had a strip wash, using the icy clear water. Just once or twice, on a warm summer morning, I joined him for this taste of the outdoor life, but we stopped the practice when the water grew brown and murky as the container rusted, a home for wriggling larvae and water fleas.

One Sunday I was standing on tiptoe amongst the roses on the trellis, peering over the rim of the rain butt. I was agitating larvae by banging the inside of the rain butt with a claw hammer borrowed from Dad's workshop. Mike, quite naturally, wanted to see into the rain butt too, but there was not room for both of us on the trellis frame so I told him to go away – impolitely, no doubt. Too busy banging the rusty container with the hammer, I failed to notice Mike clambering up beside me until he tugged at my arm. As I turned to shout at him I lost my balance and my feet slipped from the trellis frame. The claw of the claw hammer caught on the rim of the butt, so that as I fell to the ground I brought it toppling onto me. Mike fell too, but tumbled away from the danger. The butt struck me on the forehead, emptying its cold, rusty contents over my entire body. Mike stood there open-mouthed, halfway between an excuse and an apology, as I stood up and ran to the back door of the house, my tears indistinguishable from bloodied and rusty rainwater.

I must have been a frightening sight for Mum as she looked up from the kitchen sink. Once my face had been towelled dry and the extent of my injuries assessed, she calmed me down, removed my wet clothes, wrapped me in a bath towel and telephoned for an ambulance. Six stitches, two ambulance rides and three hours later I was in bed with a sore head, hot-water bottle and no tea. Mike got the blame, as usual, although this was one rare occasion when he was not guilty. He has probably forgotten the incident, but I carried a permanent reminder of that rusty rain butt for the rest of my life, a tiny scar on my forehead.

One Sunday afternoon, two or three summers later, another ambulance called, the neighbours peeped from behind their net curtains, and their children crowded around the ambulance doors to see who was stretchered beneath the red blanket. Needless to say, it was me again, staring at them staring at me. Twenty-four hours later I was home in bed with a sore head, hot-water bottle and no tea. Mike got the blame, as usual, although on this particular occasion he was lucky not to have killed me.

We had been playing with our trolleys, taking turns to push each other round the little green in front of our house. Most boys built themselves a trolley at least once, usually basing it on a set of redundant pram wheels. Everything about our trolleys was primitive, from the brakes – usually a shoe scuffed against the ground – to the orange-box driver's seat. The most primitive and most lethal feature was, without doubt, the steering system. If the trolley's wheels and sub-frame came from the same pram, the wheels were fixed and the trolley could only be steered by its pusher. You only ever drove a fixed-axle machine if you had complete trust in your pusher. Mike and I always built trolleys with front wheels which swivelled.

With the 'safer' design you had a choice of three steering methods. Firstly, you could sit in the seat and steer with the aid of a rope attached to the two ends of the front axle. A little more dangerous was sitting in the same position and steering with your feet, which were placed on the axle. The most dangerous, death-defying style of steering was to lie on your tummy facing forward and place your hands on the front axle. In this position you risked the loss of all the fingers on your right hand whenever you turned right, and similar amputation of the left-hand digits when executing a left-hand turn.

The Pegg trolley was being steered by my feet and pushed by my brother in a race against some other boys. After a few laps we were in the lead, but not by much so I didn't want a pit stop. I refused to change places with Mike, instead urging him to pro-pel me 'Faster! Faster!' I meant faster on the three straight sections of the course, not the corners. On the shortest straight, which ran from our gate up to the telegraph pole near the road, my infuriated brother found an extra gear and accelerated like a racehorse with a wasp up its arse, out of control and whinnying hysterically. I had only moments to think something like, 'The little git's going to kill me,' but no time to avoid the onrushing road. The trolley leapt off the pavement, the back wheels clipping the kerb half a second before the front wheels hit the gravelled surface of Stafford Road, spilling me out of the driver's seat and into Mount Vernon Hospital. It was lucky, I suppose, that I hadn't been hit by a car as I ploughed into the road. Fortunately for me, unfortunately for my brother, I lived to steer another trolley around the racetracks of Ruislip Gardens.

Much later, when I was about eighteen, I was at Mount Vernon Hospital again on a Sunday, but as a visitor and not a patient. Julie, in her usual dramatic fashion, had been admitted for an emergency appendectomy. One minute she was at home, washing Carol Pugh's hair, and almost before you could say 'a sachet of Silvikrin shampoo' sixty-six times she was showing off stitches in a hospital bed.

Mum was Julie's first visitor. 'I've brought some magazines,' she said, dropping *Honey*, *Nova*, *Queen* and *She* on Julie's bed. To be precise, on Julie's stitches. 'A little light reading for you,' she joked, completely unaware of what she'd just done. Julie recounted this incident when Ros and I visited later, laughing so much she almost unstitched her surgeon's needlework.

Dad often missed his Sunday tea in pursuit of overtime. At different times he was on an exhibition fit-up with 'Stage Decor', supervising a get-in at one of his own theatres, or assisting another carpenter at another theatre – another opening, another show. In addition to these regular overtime assignments, there were the more unusual jobs like building truck bodies for Jack Coales or fitting out Donald Albery's yacht.

Sometimes Mike and I went along to help Dad and earn ourselves some extra pocket money. I especially remember the Sundays spent at Coales's Garage near the Hammersmith flyover, because it was icily cold and we had to work outside. We only kept frostbite at bay by regularly running warm water from the car wash over our fingers, and we kept going with flasks of hot Campbell's vegetable soup and garlic sausage sandwiches supplied by Mum. Further occasional respite from the biting wind came when we sheltered inside a forecourt Skoda, courtesy of a sympathetic sales manager.

Nowadays Skodas are an over-used target for any aspiring and unoriginal stand-up comedian, but in 1962 the British motor industry provided enough comedy material for everyone from Butlin's Redcoat to Billy Cotton. Skodas were then a rare sight on British roads, and sitting inside one on a freezing Sunday afternoon it was easy to see why. Everything about those Skoda Estelles bore witness to the failure of Eastern European state enterprise, from the sparse and functional instrument panel, through the ill-matched, misfitted plastic and vinyl interior trim, to the drab and uneven paintwork. The Renault 4 Dad drove at that time seemed sophisticated by comparison. Thank goodness Jack Coales's offers of a discounted Skoda in return for converting trucks never tempted Dad away from his obsession with Renault cars.

According to my memory, it was on a Sunday that I received a 'belting' for the last time. Mike and I were often hit by Dad when we got into trouble, and we used to be in trouble a lot. We fought like Arab and Jew almost daily, Mum's only peace-keeping force being the threat of 'Wait 'til your father gets home.' When he got home we discovered exactly what the weight was. It was a master carpenter's palm across the backside, delivered with all the accuracy and force that comes from years of driving two-inch ovals into wood with three precision blows of a claw hammer. To be fair to Dad, and to save the NSPCC unnecessary retrospective investigative work, we usually deserved what we got.

My last-recalled 'belting' was most undeserved, however, and was earned in the following way. My long-time friend Barry Clegg had left his Roman Catholic secondary modern school a few months earlier, minus any paper qualifications but with, I suspect, many prayers of grateful thanks from nuns, teachers and ancillary staff. Barry was one of those boys for whom school is only an adventure playground rehearsal for the real world assault course that they know awaits them.

After working at Wall's East Acton factory since waving the nuns farewell, Barry had saved enough money to buy himself an expensive and professional-looking SLR camera. At least, he had made the initial down-payment and was now a member of the live-now–pay-later society.

Barry brought his camera up to our house to show me, and to invite me to join him on location. I didn't need much persuasion to drag me from History homework so I slipped my jacket from the coat rack in the hall, shouted 'Bye!' to my parents in the front room and was out of the house before anyone could say 'Where you off to?'

We were off to photograph aeroplanes at RAF Northolt. Barry and I had been on the airfield many times, climbing over old planes which had been abandoned near the River Pinn. We'd cannibalized a Gloster Meteor, an Avro Anson and several Dakotas, carrying home shattered tachometers, lengths of cable or pieces of cockpit trim to swap for cigarette cards and piles of old comics. We'd read the Ministry of Defence warning notices posted around the airfield perimeter, and had often been chased away by uniformed men in Land Rovers. However, it was so easy to get onto the airfield that we always considered our acts of trespass as nothing more than an extension of the war games we used to play in the fields and woods between Ruislip Gardens and Ickenham. By the time of the photographic location shoot we'd long since abandoned our war games, but the security at RAF Northolt was still so non-existent that we could never have equated our bit of harmless photography with espionage.

After climbing over an eight-foot gate, which wasn't electrified or crowned with barbed wire, we strolled casually to the nearest taxiway. We weren't aware of observation towers or minefields as Barry pointed his camera at a group of hangars and three or four parked Dakotas. Using the zoom lens, he was able to see clearly the faces of the men loading the aeroplanes. When I pointed the camera at the control tower, focused and snapped, we had a record of the number of air-traffic controllers on duty on a Sunday afternoon. When Barry panned across the horizon he spotted a Land Rover driven by a man wearing a blue uniform. Sitting next to him was another uniformed man who was talking into his hand. When they got nearer, and Barry adjusted the focus, he saw that both men wore white armbands. 'MPs,' he declared without emotion, as if he was identifying two sparrows on a bird table.

I really don't know why Barry and I were treating the rapidly-approaching Military Policemen with such disdain. In the past we'd have run a sub-four-minute mile at the first sight of a security patrol, but that day we just stood and smiled at the two men, even photographing them as they stepped from their vehicle.

'And what are you two up to?' asked a three-striped uniform.

'Just trying out my mate's new camera,' I replied. 'Any chance of getting closer to those Daks over there?' I enquired with all the naivety of a blindfolded vegan speaking at a Master Butchers' banquet.

The stripeless uniform looked incredulously at his colleague before playing along. 'Sure you can. Hop in.' He nodded at the Land Rover and in we hopped, with all the arrogant confidence of two blind drunk master butchers offering themselves as fraternal delegates to the annual conference of militant vegans.

Of course we never got a closer look at the DC3s, only a visit to an interview room for a brief interrogation.

Who is your section leader?

Where did you bury your parachutes?

Do the names of Peter and Helen Kroger mean anything to you?

Can you account for your movements on the day of the Bay of Pigs invasion?

Have you ever worn or purchased an enamel CND badge?

Do you have in your possession any art history books written by someone called Blunt?

How many sugars in your tea?

Have you ever sung along at a Pete Seeger concert?

What colour is the Red Flag?

Where is your safe house?

My tea tasted strange, much too sweet for just one sugar. I was unable to prevent myself revealing my address. After Barry's camera had been unloaded and his film confiscated in the interest of national security, we were formally warned against contacting the Soviet embassy and told never again to take photographs on Ministry of Defence property. The two arresting MPs then drove us back to Stafford Road and marched us up to our respective front doors.

'Apprehended them in a strictly restricted area, engaged in activity contravening Appendix 9, paras 3 to 17 inclusive, of the Official Secrets Act,' our parents were informed. Barry's dad was snoring open-mouthed on the settee in the Cleggs' front room, dreaming of owning a brewery, so Mrs Clegg – proudly Irish Republican from silver grey hair to tiny, tired feet – feigned contrition on her front step.

'I'll sort him out right enough, officers. The divil won't know what's hit him when I get him inside,' she humbled herself before the uniforms. Barry was officially handed over to his mother and disappeared down the unlit hallway into the kitchen.

My dad was not, unfortunately, asleep in our front room. Alerted by the Land Rover drawing up outside his house, he was already at the front door to usher inside without delay the criminal and escort party. No public reading of charges or washing of laundry for him, and no false apologies to follow the detailing of my crime, either. Dad's own wartime service with the Royal Air Force meant that he treated Military Policemen more respectfully than Barry's mum. He stood as still and stiff as a sentry while the events leading up to my arrest were recalled. He then pushed me up the stairs in the direction of my bedroom and saw the MPs to the front door, echoing Mrs Clegg's earlier promise to 'sort me out' as they marched down our path and back towards their Land Rover.

Barry and I, innocent partners in crime, fared differently in the treatment we received. My protestations about wrongful arrest and accusations of RAF incompetence merely made my father angrier and compounded the shame that the Military Police had visited upon his home. I was duly sorted out, but how harshly I cannot recall. I can only imagine that too-sweet tea with two MPs in an interview room at RAF Northolt would have been more pleasant.

Fortunately for Barry Clegg, his mum had no intention of sorting out her son for making Ministry of Defence security look foolish. Indeed, the first thing she sorted out for Barry was a cup of tea and two slices of margarined toast. Later that evening, her husband down at the Bell with a beer, she sat in the front room with her two daughters and three rebel sons, switched off *Beat the Clock* and told tales of her own County Cork childhood, of all the uniforms she'd run away from. 'Niver give meself up like him, though,' she gently chided Barry, her tired eyes suddenly asmile with schoolgirl mischief.

When Dad worked on Sundays at Stage Decor we sometimes had a 'Cockney tea' after he got home. Somewhere in Walworth he bought most of the ingredients – cockles, winkles, brown shrimps, a few whelks, some prawns – and Mum prepared a pile of brown bread and butter, made a pot of tea and sterilized half a dozen needles while we set the table. When everything and everyone was ready Dad reminded us how to use the pins on the winkles, and how to 'top 'n' tail' the prawns. He also warned us not to inspect too closely the cockles before popping them into our mouths. Lastly, we were discouraged from eating too many prawns, these being the most expensive items on the menu and meant for adult consumption only. We didn't need warning off the whelks, those ugly slug-alikes being very welcome to slide exclusively down Dad's throat with no envious glances from the rest of us, but we were unhappy about the imposition of prawn quotas, especially when Dad concocted a creamy sauce in which he cooked them. 'Too rich for children' was his reason for limiting us to a minute portion while he scoffed most of them. He said exactly the same thing, I remember, when someone posted us clotted cream from Devon or Cornwall, always adding that it tasted 'well past its best' in a vain attempt to placate us.

Anyway, while he and Mum enjoyed the prawns we got stuck into the shrimps, sometimes not bothering to pinch off heads or tails in our haste to consume as many as possible before Dad finished his prawns. I always had more than my fair share of winkles and cockles, too, but not through greed. Mike never had the patience needed for the delicate extrication of winkle from shell and after half a dozen failures turned his attention to the ready-prepared cockles, leaving Julie and me to enjoy winkles. Julie never heeded Dad's advice about examination of cockles, inspecting them with the same mixture of disgust and intrigue that she normally applied to the contents of her nose on the tip of her index finger. She made herself shrimp and winkle sandwiches, leaving the rest of the cockles to Mike and me.

Mum always greeted our 'Cockney teas' with mixed emotions, happy that she had little to do in the way of preparation but less pleased about the taste and texture of the seafood on offer. This ambivalence went right back to her courting days, when she was taken to Sunday tea at Dad's house for the first time and confronted with not only several strange Peggs but also a table swimming with an even stranger marine family. Nana Pegg explained how everything could be eaten and enjoyed but Mum, understandably shy and nervous on her first visit to her boyfriend's home, listened with polite incomprehension. None of Nana Pegg's instructions registered.

Tea was p
                    o
                        u
                            r
                                e
d, sweetened, stirred, sipped;
bread passed, side-plated, folded, eaten, replaced;
winkles tinkled onto plates, pins poked, wrists twisted,
shells emptied, curly contents carefully consumed, eyes
                                        piled plateside;
                fresh tea sent for, allowed to stand;
    sweet shrimps and pink prawns pinched clean,
                popped in mouths, savoured, swallowed;
more tea p
                    o
                        u
                            r
                                e
d, milked, sugared, stirred and left to cool;
cockles called for, passed politely, slid from dish,
                vinegared, peppered, disappeared;
        whelks braved, eyes closed, gulped down;
    around the table tales told while Peggs laughed
                and just occasionally a Foster smiled.

When it was over, when the last half-slice of bread had

47

been claimed, the last teacup drained, and when only the debris remained, Nana Pegg asked my mum if she had enjoyed her first 'Cockney tea'.

'Yes, thank you,' she fibbed politely, swallowing a final prawn. 'I must have enjoyed it,' she elaborated, 'because there's nothing left.' And she pointed proudly at the red rambling roses which decorated her plate. Every Pegg nose also pointed at Mum's empty plate, then Mum's innocent face, her clean plate, her reddening face, her plate, her face.

'You mean you ate everything?' Nana Pegg enquired. 'Everything? The heads, the tails, the shells, the eyes?'

Mum giggled nervously, noticing for the first time the remains on everyone else's plate. 'Not the winkle shells, I never ate them,' she defended herself. 'They're here in my saucer. I'm not that silly. I wouldn't eat them.' She'd eaten virtually everything save the rambling roses, though. Mum had crunched her way through three winkle eyes and an unspecified number of unpeeled prawns, too nervous and embarrassed to look up from her plate and observe what the others were doing.

'Never mind, Margaret,' consoled Nana Pegg. 'You'll know next time.'

She did know next time, but every next time was a painful reminder of that very first 'Cockney tea'.

On Sunday afternoons between 1966 and 1969 I ate most of my teas at 10 Charlbury Road, Ickenham, with Ros and her family. We sat in the lounge, round an open fire in the winter, and helped ourselves from a selection of sandwich-making ingredients and home-made cakes. There was always cheese and ham, tomatoes, cucumber, lettuce, Branston Pickle and mango chutney, Marmite and jam; sometimes there was beetroot, coleslaw, cold potatoes and cold meat. While the others made themselves one or two rounds of sandwiches, I usually built four or five generously-filled doorsteps which I was still enjoying when the others were on the cake course. Ros's mum made delicious cakes of diverse variety – fruit cake, fruit loaf, sticky bread, jam sponge, cream sponge, fairy cakes and scones – but best of all was 'Aunty Flo's Chocolate Cake'. No matter how much I had already eaten I always left room for at least two pieces of that chocolate cake. It was such a favourite of mine that when Ros's parents moved from Ickenham to Backwell I wrote a poem mourning its disappearance from my life. It wasn't long before I was trekking down to Somerset, though, in pursuit of chocolate cake and girlfriend.

When Ros and I started going out I used to work on Saturdays, selling shoes in Oxford Street by day and moving scenery at the Piccadilly Theatre by night, so Sunday was the only day when we could spend time together. Sometimes we went to the cinema, the Embassy in Ruislip, the Regal or Odeon in Uxbridge; occasionally we went ten-pin bowling at North Harrow; but mostly we took Goolah, the family Labrador, for long walks across the nearby golf course. If we returned home late from any of our excursions and Ros's parents and Denise had long since finished their tea, we ate in the kitchen while they watched television or read the *Observer* in the lounge. Here in the kitchen, with all the usual choices displayed on the red Formica-topped foldaway table that would later live in all our homes, I made myself even more and even fuller sandwiches, followed by a selection of cakes and accompanied by at least two pots of tea. After we had washed up and tidied the kitchen we sat in the lounge to watch television and give my tea a chance to go down before I bade my farewells and ran like the wind to catch the last train from West Ruislip. Quite often I arrived at the top of the hill near the station just in time to see the train disappearing in the direction of Ruislip Gardens.

Beaten by that sixth sandwich, third slice of cake and last cup of tea, I sat to get my breath and massage away the stitch in my side before beginning the long walk home.

GARDENERS' TALES

After I was born at Park Royal Hospital on 27 January 1948 Mum and Dad took me back to my grandparents' house in Eastfields Road, Acton, where we lived for just under two years before moving to Ruislip Gardens. Recollections of Acton stem from later visits, made after my grandfather died and before Nana Foster returned to live in County Durham. Her house was a three-bedroomed, mid-terrace, pebbledashed one, similar to thousands of houses on hundreds of estates which were developed either side of the Western Avenue in the 1930s. There was a small sunny front garden which faced a park and playground, and a slightly longer, narrow back garden with a paved yard and outhouse area which lay under the shadow of the roof. One outhouse was a coalshed and one might have been a WC, but I could be mixing this grandparental home with others that were visited later, so the outside toilet may be a figment of an overactive imagination. I definitely remember that there was an inside bathroom, though, because it was once used by my Uncle Jack as a brewery, the bath filled with fermenting beer for weeks on end. Nana Foster, never keen on alcoholic beverages, might have been expected to scold Jack for transforming her bathroom. He was always her favourite child, though, so she imitated the three brass monkeys polished and pinned to the wall in her hall, neither seeing nor hearing nor speaking any evil.

Dad and Jack were drinking pals so it's inevitable that one of my memories of my uncle features a pub. Shortly before Uncle Jack and Aunt Peggy emigrated to Australia in 1955 I went with them, Mum and Dad and Julie to a

51

pub on the Western Avenue, just up the hill from Gipsy Corner junction, where I had a bottle of lemonade, a straw and crisps – the standard fare for keeping children happy outside pubs. Michael was probably asleep in his pram outside Nana's front door while she cooked Sunday lunch of roast lamb, boiled new potatoes, freshly-podded garden peas, boiled carrots, gravy and Nana's own recipe finely-chopped mint sauce, followed by tinned fruit salad and a family block of Wall's Neapolitan ice cream which we bought on our way back from the pub. With their meal the men probably drank the last of Jack's home-brewed beer, Peggy a gin and tonic, my mum a light ale, the children fizzy orange made with crystals, Nana Foster a glass of water. Later we waved goodbye to Jack and Peggy, wishing them luck and promising to visit Australia one day soon; Dad and Nana cried but Mum kept her tears for a less public moment; Julie and I licked the ice-cream carton clean, wondering what the tears were for; Michael was still asleep in his pram, probably dreaming of earlier emigrants to Australia.

My other memory of Uncle Jack takes me to a large naval mess at Portsmouth in 1954, Jack and Dad with a cup of something and an endless supply of duty-free cigarettes, Julie and I with a plate of the creamiest, jammiest buns it has ever been my pleasure to consume. Years later I often bought the best doughnuts in England, from Karl's in Hill Road, Clevedon, for the children I taught. In fact, when I left my favourite school, Birdwell in Long Ashton, on my last morning I visited every classroom and gave every child and adult a doughnut. The image of a whole school happily devouring more than one hundred doughnuts doesn't, however, excite me as much as the memory of my own modest half-dozen jam splits.

Uncle Jack became a Chief Petty Officer in the Royal Navy, based at Gosport, I think, and later transferred to the Royal Australian Navy with the same rank. He once told us that he had been offered a commission but had turned it down because he thought that his mess bills would be too high. Bearing in mind his fondness for beer I suppose that may have been right but I suspect that he, like his brother and sister, lacked self-confidence to further his career, preferring instead to stay securely where he was. I am not criticizing his lack of ambition, though. How could I? In my own career I never wanted to be elevated to the status of head or deputy head, even though I thought that I could do the job just as well as most of those I saw in positions of responsibility.

Uncle Jack retired from the Australian Navy in the early 1960s. He received a pension from them which, together with one from the Royal Navy, must have made him reasonably well-off for a retired man. I doubt whether his combined pensions would have kept him in beer money, though, so he soon got himself another full-time job as a librarian at Sydney University, where he could indulge his passion for books and, I suspect, avail himself of cheap beer at various college bars. Unhappily, the years of smoking duty-free, naval ration, full-strength cigarettes caught up with Uncle Jack and he died of cancer, after a lengthy period of illness, on 21 October 1972.

Julie was born on 16 July 1949, while we were still living at Eastfields Road with my grandparents. In December of that year we four Peggs moved to a new semi-detached council house on the Ruislip Gardens estate. According to my mum, Nana Pegg scrubbed the house from top to bottom before we moved in. We arrived at the house in the dark, I remember, probably after my dad had finished work. We hadn't much furniture to start with, but the house itself had two inside toilets, a bathroom, a large back garden and fields beyond the back fence. It also had a kitchen, two rooms downstairs, a hallway, three bedrooms, two coal sheds and a further shed for garden tools, but it was the two toilets which fascinated me, the beer-free bathroom which obviously impressed me, and the back garden and fields which excited me.

I liked living at the top of Stafford Road, surrounded by friendly neighbours, neat gardens and brightly-painted front doors. Most residents cared for their homes and the environment, so there were few front gardens littered with old prams, rusting cars, newspaper pages and crisp packets, which are the hallmarks of most council estates I've seen.

The secret of 'The Gardens' was its scale. Unlike places where I've worked in both Bristol and London, our estate had well-marked boundaries which stopped it merging with nearby developments. There was only one point of access and egress, just off West End Road opposite the Central Line station; the River Pinn formed one long boundary, with RAF Northolt beyond the river; fields ran behind our back garden and continued as far as the river one way and out to Ickenham the other; the estate consisted of only a few roads, a couple of crescents and Acorn Grove; just under half of the houses were 'private', mostly owner-occupied but a few were rented.

A further important ingredient was continuity of occupation. Most families stayed there for many years, often moving to a different-sized home on the estate as children were either born or married and moved away. Today many houses are still occupied by the original residents, some having been bought under the right-to-buy scheme. Unfortunately, many have been 'improved' by families with three cars and a penchant for entrance porches, lean-to extensions and replacement windows. Front gardens which once contained nothing more outrageous than a privet hedge and a diamond-shaped lawn are now paved with reconstituted Cotswold stone slabs, each garden having its own wishing well and ornamental pond. By the Georgian front door is a Regency coach lamp and a black wrought-iron proclamation of upward mobility, 'Casa Mia', 'Puerto Pollensa' or 'Kevantracey'.

The council estates of Mottingham, Dagenham and Woolwich which I knew when I was training at Avery Hill College in London may also have been 'improved' in recent years, but I doubt it. These estates seemed to me huge and heartless, inhabited by neighbourless strangers; shuffling old ladies struggling with a few tins and a 'small white sliced' in an old wicker trolley; mums with too many toddlers packed into pushchairs; too many toddlers with runny noses and dirty dummies; groups of absenting pupils from the local comprehensive camped outside a graffitied community centre, consenting schoolgirls and dissenting schoolboys kicking their heels and spitting in the wind; packs of roaming dogs, skipping through unfenced gardens to dustbin compound, crapping from shopping precinct to children's playground. After my training I taught in Hartcliffe, part of a sprawling development on the southern edge of Bristol, and was able to observe more closely some of the aspects of council-estate living which were commonplace in the seventies but rare in the Gardens when I lived there.

Many Hartcliffe back gardens adjoined our school field so it was easy to inspect them as I patrolled on my duty days. Just a few contained roses, dahlias, chrysanthemums, lanky competing sunflowers; most featured a cracked and subsided concrete path; each had its plastic washing line draped between two leaning lengths of scaffold pole; for every thirteen gardens you could count on counting twelve mongrel dogs, all equally scraggy, yappy, thin, unhappy, each hinting at an Alsatian parent; every thirteenth garden had a much-mended fence, behind which an agitated Alsatian called Bruce barked out his escape plans; some of the gardens contained an ornamental pond, once home to eight exotic carp and an angling gnome but now, plastic lining long since punctured, last resting place for a fridge door, bed frame, bicycle pump, a rabbit hutch without a roof, a kitchen stool with two legs. Many of the gardens had piles of old bricks, mounds of assorted scrap metal, stacks of salvaged timber – all collected and kept, presumably, so that in the event of earthquake or hurricane a shanty town could be speedily built upon the ruins of Hartcliffe.

Despite the efforts of some residents to keep their gardens neat and tidy, Hartcliffe was a scruffy place. Litter blew along the streets, and where hedges and fences still stood it gathered as perpetual discouragement for even the keenest gardener. During my travels around Bristol I discovered other areas which were, in my opinion, worse than Hartcliffe. Highridge was rougher, Lawrence Weston bleaker, Knowle West noisier. The huge estates of London and Bristol were menacing and dispiriting in a way that Ruislip Gardens could never have been. It was small, it was friendly, it was clean; I felt secure and happy; I belonged. If I'd been brought up in a place like Hartcliffe I'm sure that I would be alienated and resentful, have litter in the front garden, a fridge door in an empty pond, and own an agitated Alsatian called Bruce.

I don't want to paint Ruislip Gardens as the perfect place in which to live. It had its share of litter, old bike frames, uneven pavements and various other landscape blots, but there were no graffitied walls, vandalized fences, smashed windows or packs of crapping roamers. Most front gardens were simple and tidy, some were colourful, and a few even turned my head as I wandered through the fifties and sixties. Most back gardens were places for play and drying washing so they always had a grassed area, a path and concrete posts. Behind our back garden were fields in which we played, and from which I observed some of my neighbours in Stafford Road.

Our house was at the top end of Stafford Road, immediately next to the primary school. The soil was a heavy clay which made gardening difficult, flooded quickly when it rained and became rock-hard when it didn't. Mum was responsible for the gardens, Dad being away so much with his work. She tried to encourage us to help her but none of us was very enthusiastic. I occasionally mowed the grass or weeded the borders, but never had the patience to make a reliable assistant, so Mum was left alone to tend her roses in the front, lupins and rockery out the back. Other things survived the clay and the clumsy feet of wild children, but I have never been good with names of plants so cannot catalogue further the contents of front and back.

Beyond our back lawn was Dad's workshop, The Shed, which had a pigeon loft attached at one time. We once had six fantail pigeons, but most of them were ambushed by the Taylors' ginger cat and left dead in a pile of white feathers on the lawn. Right behind The Shed was our gypsy caravan – a full-size replica which Dad had built for a show at 'Q' Theatre and later brought home – in which we played with our friends. Our roundabout, also made by Dad, was next to the caravan; when we outgrew it, Dad tried cultivating strawberries between the spokes of the base. Potatoes and rows of cabbages were also grown in this rear section of garden, which was divided from the fields by a three-foot-high wire fence.

Our neighbours at number 67 were Mr and Mrs James and their children John (a year older than me) and Beryl (one of Julie's classmates). Both of their gardens were immaculately kept, the grass at the back being a proper lawn with straight edges and no moss or clover to offend Mr James's critical eye. Cricket matches or little girls' picnics never took place at number 67, no plastic football or skipping rope ever snapped a chrysanthemum stem. Beryl had to play 'out the front', on the pavement or the green, but John rarely played at all, especially after he went to secondary school. A pity, that, because he was a good story and joke teller and an excellent mimic. I always imagined that his dour Welsh father discouraged him from mixing freely with the less-refined boys on the estate, preferring his son to learn the art of privet-trimming.

Those front and back hedges were not only Mr James's pride and joy, they served as the last line of defence against the real world which appeared to make him so uneasy. He rarely smiled or spoke to anyone, save to warn children away from his hedge or green Austin 1100. His wife, only marginally more communicative, was short and plump to his tall and thin, a rolypoly lady who had once argued with my mum and could never thereafter bring herself to acknowledge any of us who lived next door. To be fair, Mum behaved the same way. The husbands also played their silent part, so an air of animosity drifted between our two homes for over twenty years, hovering malevolently just above Mr James's hedge. Somehow we children managed to co-exist fairly amicably through all the years of our parents' immaturity. Eventually, long after John and Beryl, Julie, Mike and I had married and moved away, some semblance of normal neighbourliness was restored when Mr James died after a long illness. The two women began to chat across the privet hedge and Dad helped Mrs James with things like dripping taps and broken lawnmowers. Such a shame that it needed a bereavement to cut through all that accumulated animosity.

At 69 Stafford Road lived Charlie Taylor, his wife, and their three daughters, Pat, Diane and Jean. Their gardens were always neat and tidy but never particularly colourful; the only outstanding individual feature was the rose trellis that Charlie, a carpenter, built halfway down the back garden. Jean played with Julie a lot but the older girls had different friends who lived away from Ruislip Gardens. When they were first teenagers they drove us mad with their incessant playing of Everly Brothers records, especially 'Cathy's Clown' and 'Bye Bye Love'. Not long afterwards they began to drive boyfriends wild in *True Romance* clichéd style. I had no interest in girls at this time but Bardotesque Pat and dark-haired Diane impressed me enough to distract me from my *Beezer* and *Beano* whenever they sunbathed in their back garden.

When they left the Manor Secondary Modern School Pat got a 'factory job' with Sanderson at Perivale and Diane worked as a trainee dental nurse. One of Diane's boyfriends was an Australian dentist who drove an MG Midget; later they married and moved to New Zealand; later still she contracted Multiple Sclerosis and was nursed by her husband. Pat and Jean both married local boys and lived local lives, less exotic than Diane's but with happier endings, I hope.

Mr Draper lived at number 71 with his wife, daughter Pamela and sons Norman and Peter. Sometimes I used to be driven to school in Mr Draper's immaculately-kept silver and burgundy Ford Prefect, but only if I promised not to put my scruffy shoes on his immaculately-kept upholstery. That car was his proudest possession, and he devoted at least two hours each Sunday morning to washing, leathering, polishing and admiring it. The only rival for Mr Draper's attention was his garden.

Mr Draper spent more time caring for his garden than anyone else I ever knew, and it showed. His lawns were not quite as perfect as Mr James's, but his roses were as healthy as Percy Thrower's and his fruit trees as prolific as any nurseryman's. Everything in his garden was properly pruned, correctly positioned and perfectly proportioned. If there had ever been a Ruislip Gardens Gardener Competition, Mr Draper would have been undisputed champion, his sideboard groaning under the weight of a perfectly symmetrical display of regularly polished electro-plated nickel silver trophies.

My friend Brian Beasley lived at 75 Stafford Road. His father was an insurance agent, and one of the few men to stick a Vote Conservative poster in his window at election time. Mrs Beasley, like nearly every married woman then, was a housewife; unlike anyone else in

Stafford Road, she owned a poodle, a black one with a *soupçon* of French sophistication in its name – Bobo. Brian's sister Janice (about ten years older than me) ran her own poodle parlour locally so Bobo was always the best-groomed, most sophisticated, right-wing dog in the Gardens.

The Beasley front garden was as conservative as Harold Macmillan – predictable, unspectacular, unimaginative, colourless, boring – the acceptable face of the insurance man presented to the passing world. The back garden, by contrast, was the anarchic setting for Brian's obsession with things mechanical, things oily, things grimy and things in pieces. Brian was very likely born with an adjustable spanner in his mouth and a suspicion of an inner tube at the end of the umbilical cord; where other babies had birthmarks Brian would have had a puncture repair patch; his mother would have powdered his bottom with French chalk and smeared his nappy rash with Swarfega; while other infants slept after lunch and *Listen With Mother*, Brian was on his back underneath his pram carrying out a 3,000-mile service. All the time I knew Brian he was building and dismantling, damaging, and repairing, his fingernails forever black, the back lawn a permanent home to frames and chains, cowhorn bars and brake pads.

Brian, a year older than me, was at Manor Secondary Modern when I went to grammar school but we remained friends until he was old enough to ride motorbikes. He was keen for me to ride pillion but, knowing how accident-prone he was, I kept making excuses until he gave up trying to tempt me. Surprisingly, I never heard of Brian coming to grief on any two-wheeled machine whereas I, in another friend's car, was later very lucky to escape serious injury in a road accident.

I last spoke to Brian in about 1968. He was dismounting an enormous Norton outside his house as I walked from work at Bourne School in South Ruislip. While he baffled me with technical data which I pretended to understand, I observed his expensive leather jacket, trousers and boots.

'Must have cost a fortune,' I said, nodding at his boots. He told me how much of a fortune, and then removed his leather gauntlets to show off their quality. 'Spanish,' I remarked, inspecting the label, and Brian explained where he'd bought them and how much they'd cost. I was just thinking how much cleaner and smarter Brian had become when I saw his hands and fingernails – as black and grimy as they had ever been. He saw that I saw and we grinned at each other.

'Still messing about, I see.'

'Yes,' he agreed. 'Still messing about.'

Next door to the Beasleys lived the Lucas family, tall Mister and short Missus, David, Irene and Yvonne. Mr Lucas drove buses for London Transport when he first moved into number 77 but later became a chauffeur for an oil company, and parked a large black Humber Snipe Automatic outside his house each night. Whenever he saw me walking up or down Stafford Road in bad weather he would stop and offer me a lift, once driving me into London and saving me 3/6d, or whatever it cost at that time. Mr Lucas was no gardener, leaving the tidying of his plain back and front patches to his diminutive wife and two daughters.

The Woodman family lived at number 79, jolly parents with handsome Alan, plump Cathy, quiet Michael and late arrival Keith. Cathy Woodman was one of Julie's schoolfriends, although not one of her best. Julie admits that she only played with Cathy to get near the handsome Alan and when he started bringing home a regular girl-friend Julie's friendship with Cathy ceased abruptly.

Alan worked at Saitch's Farm in Ickenham after he left school at fifteen, walking there daily across the fields to the farm in Sharp's Lane. He thus became one of the 'enemy', since the gangs with which Mike and I ran used

61

Saitch's fields as the battleground for our war games and the course for tracking. Sometimes we also indulged in less innocent pastimes like rolling through cereal fields and setting fire to drying straw. Saitch and his workers knew the identity of the Gardens guerrillas – Clegg, Pegg, Fox and Williams – and gave chase whenever they saw us. I remember being hunted at speed through the woods one afternoon, caught and swiped heftily round the head because, my captor said, I looked as if I was about to do something wrong. For once, though, I was not intent on sabotaging Saitch's agricultural activities but had been on my way to my favourite pond where I had hoped to catch some water boatmen and great diving beetles for the freshwater aquarium in my classroom at school. It wasn't Alan Woodman who chased and bashed me but Saitch's longest-serving labourer, a man whose muscly arms and rugged features reminded me of the graveyard convict from *Great Expectations*. He certainly scared the Charles Dickens out of this young Pip.

My friend Barry Clegg lived at number 83. Barry's back garden was the scruffiest I knew, bare earth in the middle and jungle grass by the fences, bonfire remains on the bare earth and ghastly unmentionables hidden in the jungle. The back fence had been sat and swung on, then stamped and bounced upon within days of its erection, and now served only to trip up unsuspecting visitors or gang members with a poor memory. Mike often fell at this hurdle, as did Barry's thick-witted youngest brother Nigel. Coal-shed doors swung crazily in any gentle wind, catches and hinges all about to croak their last creak after much abuse from the Clegg boys. These coal sheds contained damp magazines and newspapers, lengths of string, broken flowerpots, buckets without bottoms, several warped tennis racquets, an old black pram – everything bar the kitchen sink and coal, in fact. The dismembered remains of a bike had been unceremoniously scattered everywhere, a chain and a set of front forks lurking in the long grass and awaiting the blundering arrival of Nigel or Mike.

The back garden was made even more of a minefield by the traps so randomly set by the Cleggs' dog, an energetic long-haired mongrel which looked as if its grandparents could have been an experienced Sealyham, a permissive Old English sheep dog, an aggressive Irish wolfhound and a consenting Highland terrier. That dog's name eludes me now in a way that we could never elude it then. Whenever we wanted to do something without the dog Barry locked it in his kitchen and we would escape at speed to the old swimming pool near the train sheds, to the woods or even as far as Saitch's junkyard in Sharp's Lane. Eventually, though, Mrs Clegg would let the dog out and it picked up our trail quicker than any Comanche scout. Barry and I would be on the point of doing some naughty deed – hiding behind bushes and about to lob crab apples at a couple kissing in the grass, or scrumping pears from an Ickenham orchard – when that dog would appear, bark at Barry and give away our position. 'Run for it!' we'd yell simultaneously, dashing for one of our secret refuges without daring to look behind us, Barry's dog yelping dementedly and snapping at our ankles. After we had got our breath back and checked that we were not being followed, we would return to Barry's house and lock ourselves in the kitchen this time, leaving the dog to dig holes and lay mines in the back garden while we made ourselves beans on toast and mugs of instant coffee.

Barry's back garden was a mess, it's true, but not unique. Many back gardens, especially those in which large numbers of children were confined, suffered excess wear and tear although it's worth repeating that none was as worn and torn as the Cleggs'.

Their front garden was most definitely unique, however, being fuller and more fantastically flowery than anything west of Kew and left of Wonderland. Mrs Clegg designed, built, planted and tended her front patch despite the combined distractions of two daughters and destructions of four men, her Wild Bunch sons and Lone Stranger husband. I'm sure that Mrs Clegg's hanging baskets represented a wry floral warning to the family cowboys but Nigel still tripped on a roller skate and crushed her tiny seedlings, Rolston parked his track bike against her lupins, Barry deadheaded her live roses with his Bowie knife, and Mr Clegg wove a path from 'Bell' to bed via whatever his sons had failed to destroy. In the face of so many garden pests a lesser mortal would have capitulated, but Mrs Clegg was made of sterner Western Ireland stuff and continued to nurture all manner of things in all manner of containers.

Apart from her hanging baskets she used buckets, old enamelled washing-up bowls, wooden tubs, lengths of pipe, tyres, jam jars and empty paint cans. She hammered together some rustic fencing along which she grew her roses, some of them wild ones which she'd dug up from the fields. I don't know the names of all the things that Barry's mum grew but her front garden was always interesting, especially in summer with its confusion of colour, but even in winter when it rested, waiting for spring and the gardener's quiet Gaelic singing. Even in winter, when Nigel slipped on the icy concrete path and collided with a host of frozen daffodils; when Rolston abandoned his bike at speed in the biting wind and rushed indoors to warm his numb fingers by the paraffin heater; when Barry cleared snow from the rustic fence with mighty blows from his fireman's axe; when Mr Clegg careered into the red and green plastic discs with which his wife edged her flower beds. Even after all this misfortune and abuse Mrs Clegg's front garden was guaranteed to turn the most preoccupied head.

Next door to the Cleggs lived Mrs Williams, her daughter Gloria and her son Chris. I never knew anything of Mrs Williams's circumstances but I didn't need a Community Health Care qualification to recognize that she was the poorest, unhappiest, most undernourished and unhealthiest Stafford Road resident. As far as I know, her only source of income was a daily cleaning job at the Bell, and she shuffled between there and her house looking more like a Dickensian beggar than a mid-twentieth century housewife. She always wore the same old worn shoes and threadbare overcoat; her hair was thin and barely brushed, her face gaunt and sad. She moaned quietly to herself and stared down at the pavement whenever walking in the street, as if she didn't want to confront anyone else with her miserable existence.

Mrs Williams never gardened, needless to say, having hardly enough income or energy to buy and cook food for herself and her children. I remember once going into her kitchen at midnight when a group of boys were camping in the 'first field', immediately behind our houses. It was cold in our tents and none of us could sleep so three Cleggs, two Peggs, Billy Fox and Chrissy Williams decided to have a midnight feast. The only houses with lights on were the Cleggs' and Chrissy's, so while Mike and Nigel stoked the camp fire the rest of us wandered back to search for provisons. There was no-one in the Clegg kitchen, just the smell of recently burned toast and a scene of devastated crockery in the sink to tell us that Mr Clegg had not long since stumbled up to bed. Barry found two tins of Armour baked beans – whereupon we all chorused 'Armour beans are oh so tasty' – half a pound of Echo margarine and some brown sauce lurking at the bottom of an OK bottle. Unfortunately, Barry's dad had just cremated the last of the Sunblest, and his sisters had earlier devoured an entire box of Ritz crackers that Rowley thought he had hidden at the back of the larder, so we walked next door to commandeer some bread from Chrissy's kitchen.

But when we got there the cupboards were bare, and we poor little campers had none. There was not a single thing to eat in that kitchen, and no evidence of recent eating, either – no empty soup cans stood on the window sill waiting for the dustbin, no smell of cabbage or fried bacon, no dirty saucepans soaking in the sink, no breadcrumbs on the kitchen table. No wonder Chrissy Williams and his mum were so thin.

At 87 Stafford Road you could find the Paisley family, two boys, one girl and their parents. All the children were at least ten years older than me so never figured in any of my adventures, and the only memorable thing about them that I can recall concerns the younger son, Arthur. Almost every Saturday I used to walk to Grosvenor Vale, Ruislip, to watch the top local football club, Ruislip Manor, or the top local football club's reserve team. Sometimes Victor Holden and Paul Butler joined me to cheer 'Manor' in their white shirts and black shorts as they moved from league to league – London, Corinthian, Spartan, Athenian. They never won promotion, though, but resigned from one league and got elected to another. 'Manor fined again' was a regular back-page headline in the local paper as they laboured to match the status of local rivals Hayes, Uxbridge and Yiewsley.

I think I paid 9d to get in to the ground, but whenever funds were low I arrived after halftime and was admitted free. The highlight of any Saturday afternoon would have been a Manor win, but since these were as rare as my brother telling the truth the usual highlight was the mug of hot Bovril and packet of Cheddar Cheese biscuits I bought in the Social Club.

One Saturday, arriving late and savouring my hot drink behind a goalmouth, I nearly dropped Bovril plus biscuits when I realized the Manor goalie was Arthur Paisley. I hadn't even known he played football, let alone football for a 'big' team. He played well, too – too well to keep him at Manor for much longer and he soon moved on.

Some time later – about 1967 – Arthur hit the headlines in the local papers when he saved a penalty kick in an Amateur Cup semi-final and thereby earned his team, Wealdstone, an appearance in a Wembley Stadium final. According to our local, the *Post*, Arthur was a late choice for the match, the regular first team goalkeeper being injured and failing a fitness test on the morning of the big game. (Real 'Roy of the Rovers' stuff, this!) After the penalty had been awarded (two minutes from the end of full time with the scores level, in the best Melchester tradition) Arthur is alleged to have walked up to the player preparing to take the penalty and told him, 'If you don't score from this kick then you don't deserve to get to Wembley.' The player duly took a weakly struck penalty which Arthur saved easily. ('Flung himself full length and fingertipped the ball round the post,' is how 'Tiger' would have described it.) Wealdstone won the tie after a hard-fought replay, starring Arthur once again, but when they went to Wembley he spectated from the stand, the first-choice goalie having recovered from injury just in time to displace unlucky Arthur. I think that Wealdstone had a special medal struck for him, though, as a memento of the part he played in the club's success – or was that something I once read about Melchester Rovers and Roy?

Arthur's dad was the family gardener. His preference was high, thick privet hedges which he kept neatly trimmed, and lawns which he kept closely cropped. There was little colour in either front or back patch, just a few rose bushes. Roses were a favourite of many Stafford Road gardeners because, I suppose, they were one of the few things that grew well in the unfriendly clay.

My friend Richard Ball lived next door to the Paisleys, and roses grew in his front garden, too. I can remember nothing significant about his gardens other than that the back garden was the last in Stafford Road with direct access to the fields behind. Richard climbed over his back fence to join me in various escapades, but not very often since his mother was one of many who discouraged association with the Clegg boys. Although my own mother didn't like me playing with them, Barry and his brothers were no naughtier than scores of other Ruislip Gardens boys, and less like minor criminals than certain shoplifting boys who lived not a million miles away in circumstances much more favourable than the Cleggs'. During the holidays I played with Barry Clegg quite a lot so Richard kept away, but at school we were good friends, confusing new teachers and visitors with our similar appearance – same height and build; same short grey trousers and hand-knitted sleeveless pullover; and same Adam Faith hairstyle, baybee.

Some of the episodes in this chapter may have been exaggerated slightly or embellished to create a more interesting tale, but there are also features of some gardens that I have unfortunately forgotten, and there are definitely some secrets deliberately left untold. Although question marks must accompany some of my memories, I'm happy to have recorded my thoughts about the front and back gardens in Stafford Road that I knew best. At least, I would be happy if I could rid my head of one niggling doubt, one infuriatingly elusive mystery. Remember those back fences, like the one that the Clegg brothers trampled upon, like the one that some of us climbed over on the way to adventure? Well, one of those low back fences featured in an incident which is only part-recalled by me, but which was wholly unforgettable for one young Ruislip Gardens resident.

One afternoon near the end of the summer holiday, some time between the first dog in space and the Tokyo Olympics, I was messing around in The Shed, very probably hammering nails into pieces of wood in a vain attempt to create something useful like a bookshelf, or something arty like an abstract three-dimensional sculpture. Or was I hiding in the old crab apple tree in the 'second field' from my brother and Nigel Clegg, it being their turn to be the trackers in a game of tracking? On the other hand, I might have been alone in my bedroom, listening to a reel-to-reel tape recording of Memphis Slim and painting 'The Blues Singer', one of many poster-paint creations done during an introspective period of my early teenage years. What I was doing, where and when, has no bearing on the story other than to show that I missed the drama that unfolded further down Stafford Road.

That summer afternoon, another young man was playing in his back garden with one of his friends when the friend climbed over the fence into the 'first field' and ran off towards the bare patch of ground where bonfires used to be built before Guy Fawkes night (and always lit by some mystery saboteur a few days before 5 November). The young man shouted, 'Wait for me!' and chased after his friend, hurdling the fence that divided first field from back garden. Unfortunately, the young man's hurdling technique owed rather more to Dick Emery than David Hemery, his unsuccessful attempt leaving him painfully straddled across a fence that threatened to divide rather more than first field from back garden. To cut a long story short, an ambulance came and an ambulance man unhooked hurdler from hurdle; the ambulance sped away before young man bled away, young man's mum holding young man's hand tenderly in her own; and young man holding sterile dressing very tenderly against future prospects.

Who was that young man? There are a few outside candidates but three strong favourites, all of them with good form on the flat but nervous over fences. If I was a bookmaker I'd have to give them all the same odds, something short, something appropriate, something like 2–1. Even if I could recall that name I doubt whether I'd reveal it. This particular Gardener's Tale will have to remain endless.

Far away a swallow dreams

The trees outside scratch across the sky,
    like scars.
Sparrows shiver, and dream of summer,
    and chase each other.
Autumn has gone with the goods train
    that heaves by, and the children wait
for winter which will come on the roofs
    of the next Midlands express.

Far away swallows dream of Durham summer
    and dive through Weardale mirage.
But I walk Sadly Street, kicking the last few
    leaves of autumn, while the gulls
from housetops scream abuse at me.
    The starling I loved as a child,
because it imitated the gull so well,
    picks at the bones of a tree.

When once it was summer
    the children climbed the trees.
Now they trample amongst the leaves,
    and the leaves crackle like wood burning.
They throw the leaves as high as they dare
    and try to catch them as they float down.
Old ladies with faces like shrivelled apples
    smile from behind windows memory-misted.

When the world as far as I can see
    is iced like a Christmas cake
I know that winter has swooped.
    Sparrows and starlings come begging
and the children make snowmen in Sadly Street;
    the trees are laced across the sky
and the roofs of the Midlands express are white;
    and far away a swallow dreams of Durham
    summer.

my sister flew from sydney
she smiled, she sighed
later she cried
you just look so sad she said

my sister flew from sydney
she didn't mind
my wasted hands
my tired limbs
but dared to say
what others were
afraid to see

Not waving but frowning

I never saw him, the club linesman,
Still there moaning,
Much further from the play than me,
No longer waving but frowning.

Poor sod, he was always flagging,
But banned now from the touchline.
That must have been worse for him
Than any rebuke or maximum fine.

Oh, no no no, he was too slow always,
(The crowd in the park forever moaning)
Much too far away all his life,
And not waving but frowning.

Melvin Moor

Of course he never fell in love,
But dreamed staring through ceiling to sky
Of seagulls which flew so high
They didn't care about hawks
Or boys with airguns.

He never had the courage to ask a name;
His pigeons were his only friends,
Sharing a garden shed with him
And an ancient shining tricycle
And shoe-boxes capacity-crowded with football
    programmes.

He only watched from his bedroom window,
Between the incidents in the life of Desperate Dan
His mind wandering with wonderful radio fun.
Above the storms of passion, murmurs of self-will,
A homeward-bound grammar school girl smiled.

When the words became tangled with his tongue
He wished he could be sat by the sea,
Someone alone and eating sandwiches made at home,
Writing his name in the sand with his feet
While his mind soared with the seabirds.

As she smiled shyly away he whispered her name
And traced her face on the words on the pane.
Daily, she never unlocked his garden gate
Or splashed through the puddles on the path.
Only she brought her friends to smile and wave.

On an excursion Sunday in a seaside town,
Clutching pocket money and a ticket home,
Alone on the Big Dipper, a boy with a dream;
He stood to wave at a schoolgirl he knew
And for just the space of a scream he was a
    seagull, too.

Marion's Flowers

George was always dancing then,
Up and down Old Oak Lane or
There and back on a West End train.
Flirting in and out of the limelights
Or waltzing in the clouds
On a pair of silver wings
George could say the sweetest things.
Gently twisting a sister's Liberty scarf,
'Look at Veronica Lake,' he laughed.

Carry some flowers to Crete for me, Peggy,
And drop them into the sea.
George was there once, caught in a spot,
His engine out of time with his heart.
Slow – slow – quickstep – slow
Until his heart refused to go.
Just a few steps from an airfield,
Ducane Road a distant world,
He glided into the sea.
Carry some flowers to Crete for me.

Under the bluest sky I'd ever seen,
Perfect save for a 737's distant scar,
I stepped between the Bavarians on the beach –
Women too wide for a wide-angle lens,
Men with fuel consumption figures
To match their Mercedes Benz.
Beyond the sunbeds shrouded under hotel towels,
Far from the cervelat and the madding vowels,
I laid the flowers on a retreating wave.
Later, sipping lemon tea in the shade,
I wrote a postcard home: 'Sitting here
Watching George's flowers float away.
Too hot to dance today.'

Night Moves (for Jean and Ros)

Sleeping with a shadow now,
No head upon the pillow next
Nor hand to hold,
Girls who danced to morning once
Now lie alone, wait all night
For partners. Listening
For a step they know,
Old moves upon the stairs are now
Become old stairs upon the move.

Hoping to touch, hands glide
Over icy sheets, find
Empty corners only.
Dancers sigh, rise, trip
Between old moves pinned on walls
To stir tea, turning in the kitchen
'Til the tune ends, just dancing
In the dark 'til the pain ends.

Beachy Head

Distracted by gulls, or a sudden gap in the clouds;
waving at someone far below, or the wasp above
    his head;
a boy I met and a man I never knew
flew from a clifftop.
                    Fingers crossed
inside a stranger's hand,
the boy on the river and the man lost at sea,
two pebbles dropping with one splash.

FIRST TEACHER,
AND FRIEND FOREVER

By the time you started at St Andrew's, Eleanor, I was already ill and unable to walk, so I never experienced the pleasure of taking you to school in the morning or collecting you at 'home time'. Before that I often used to drive you to Kathy, the child minder, remember? And after work it was usually me who rushed back to Clevedon and collected you. Later, when I had stopped teaching because of my illness, I occasionally picked you up from Mrs Irving's playgroup. That always gave me a lot of pleasure.

When I went to school I was never taken or collected. That was because our house in Stafford Road was right next door to Ruislip Gardens Primary School. Despite this, I rarely arrived on time. Most mornings in our house resembled a dressing-up race at the Mad Hatter's Breakfast Party so I was inevitably one of the last into the playground, still chewing toast and licking marmalade from my lips as the nine o'clock bell summoned everyone to line up in silence, in rows either side of the flagpole. When the command was given by the duty teacher we marched through doors and along corridors to our classrooms, Infants on the ground floor, Juniors up the stairs.

My first infants' teacher was Miss Byworth, the kindest and gentlest person I ever met in any school anywhere. Almost all of my last two years at Ruislip Gardens were spent in the class of Miss Astell, the most unpredictable teacher I ever encountered. Other teachers whose names spring between these two were Mrs Pavitt, who played

78

the recorder; Miss Cooper, who cycled to school and was good at rounders; and Mr Griffiths, a giant of a man whose voice was loud enough and frightening enough to silence immediately a whole playground of noisy children whenever he was on duty.

Mr Griffiths used to take the boys for football in the days before the fields behind our house were transformed into school pitches. Every Wednesday afternoon, so long as it wasn't raining, a line of boys trailed behind Mr Griffiths. We walked all the way down Stafford Road, went under the railway bridge, crossed over West End Road by the shops and crocodiled up Sidmouth Drive to the playing fields. By the time we'd tied our football boots and picked sides, our football games lasted about twenty minutes before we began the route march back to school.

In my final year at Ruislip Gardens we played just one representative football match, against Breakspear in Ickenham. We travelled on a red Underground train to West Ruislip, walked from station to school and lost 0–1. Mr Griffiths was a Welshman who knew very little about football played with a round ball so he made me captain, just because my position was centre half and the England captain of the time, Billy Wright, also played there.

If I'd never been taught by Wendy Byworth I doubt whether I would have chosen to train as a teacher. After all, I don't give many indications of enjoying my own schooldays, do I? If I'm honest I suppose that I went into teaching for two reasons. Firstly, I liked the idea of long holidays and, secondly, I wanted school to be the sort of happy, friendly workplace that only a few people, like Wendy, ever manage to create. I was not always completely successful at imparting knowledge or making my pupils work hard, but I think I helped some develop self-confidence and I hope that I amused and enthused most of them.

I was fortunate to be a member of Wendy Byworth's very first class for a number of reasons, not the least being that she selected me as a 'favourite'. Teachers try not to show favouritism but it's inevitable that they relate particularly well to some pupils. During my own teaching days I always had a fondness for lively girls and boys, pupils who could tell and take a joke. I liked such children because, I'm sure, they reminded me of the junior school boy I used to be. I don't know why Wendy Byworth selected me, Alan Fowler and Stephen Richards from her probationary year class, but she used to take us out somewhere at least once a year. When Alan moved away from the Ruislip area, Judith Walton replaced him in the lucky trio.

Wendy's parents lived in Stanmore, a few miles away, in an enormous house. Her father was a local GP and her mother ran a nursery in part of the family home. The Byworth lifestyle was completely alien to anything ever experienced by any of us. Whenever Wendy took us to meet her family we always seemed to gather in a kitchen huger than my entire house; a French au pair always seemed to be preparing vegetables in the double sink; and an elegantly-dressed, permanently calm Mrs Byworth always seemed to offer us a choice from several exotic fruit squashes, barley waters AND cordials. Compare this with our kitchen where there was barely enough room to flick a tea towel at my brother, my hard-pressed mum always seemed to be washing up in a cluttered sink and Julie had just guzzled the last drop of Sunfresh.

We usually visited the Byworth house after Wendy had taken us somewhere. She sometimes took us to a theatre but, because she knew this wasn't much of a novelty for me, also 'treated' us elsewhere. On different occasions we went to Olympia to see Bertram Mills' Circus, toured Madame Tussaud's Waxworks, rowed in Oxford and watched soldiers at Windsor Castle.

Most treats recall at least one memorable incident.

During a Christmas journey in one of Wendy's trusty Morris Minors a bolt of lightning struck the road with a frightening flash only feet from my face. In Windsor I joined in with the marching bandsmen, much to the amusement of Wendy and the other watchers. After the circus, while visiting some caged animals, Wendy got too close to a tiny monkey which grabbed her hair. Inside a theatre I was so surprised to see Anton Dolin appear in flesh-coloured tights that I blurted out loudly, 'He's got nothing on!'

Most treats also included a meal in a restaurant. When Wendy first took us out, while we were small and unsophisticated, she'd usually take us to a milk bar. We were allowed to choose anything from the menu, no expense spared. Despite this, Stephen Richards always selected egg and chips, much to everyone's amusement. I was a little more adventurous, determined to have something completely different from the food Mum served up. Perhaps Stephen Richards's mother never cooked egg and chips at home.

When we three moved on to grammar school Wendy introduced us to bigger and more expensive menus. Once we went to Lyons Corner House in Coventry Street, not very far from the Piccadilly Theatre. This might have been the same year we saw *The Mousetrap*, then in about its tenth year at the Ambassadors Theatre. Lyons Corner House was an enormous place on several floors, with different sorts of restaurants on each floor. Once before Wendy had treated us to high tea in the ground floor Tea Shoppe, where we'd queued for a table and had been served by one of Lyons's special waitresses, a 'nippy'. After *The Mousetrap*, though, we were escorted downstairs by a man in a dark suit to a reserved table in the posh basement restaurant. A trio of 'Hungarian' gypsy violinists serenaded us while we tucked into our meal. I think I ate something cooked in red wine, which was extremely adventurous for me in 1962, but Stephen Richards picked his usual. The only time I recall him not choosing egg and chips was in Simpson's in the Strand the following year, when he succumbed to pressure from a severe-looking maître d' and selected the roast rib of beef for which the restaurant was famous. That same maître d' recommended I try the real horseradish sauce, and then had a good laugh at my expense when I swallowed a huge mouthful and almost blew my head off.

Wendy only taught at Ruislip Gardens for two years, moving to a small school in Oxford next. After a few years there she became a counsellor/teacher in a comprehensive school near Reading. This surprised me since I thought she'd be too gentle and quietly-spoken to cope with stroppy adolescents, but she remained there for seven or eight years before she retrained at Bristol Methodist College and was subsequently appointed as a deaconess in London's Mile End Road.

I kept in touch with Wendy, sending Christmas cards and occasionally meeting her in Bristol, where her sister, Tessa, started the Restaurant du Gourmet with her French husband. I'd always intended to arrange a reunion of Wendy and her four 'favourites' but, like so many things I'd hoped to do, I never got round to it. About eight years ago Mrs Byworth wrote to tell me that Wendy had died after a short illness. If a Heaven is waiting for me when I die, I'm certain that Wendy will be the kindest and gentlest angel there to greet me.

SCHOOL DINNERS

In 1957 or thereabouts I think that school meals used to cost 10d a day. This wasn't a lot but Mum reckoned that she could feed herself, Julie, Mike and me for less than half a crown so we all used to go home for dinner. As we only lived next door to the school we could be sat down at the table, hands washed, knife and fork at the ready while those children who 'stayed for dinners' still queued outside the dining hall. They endured things like gristly meat, watery cabbage and lumpy mashed potato while we enjoyed home-made specialities such as cottage pie, carrots and peas; they lined up for tapioca with a splodge of jam whereas our waitress brought us whatever we liked – just as long as it was rice pudding with two splodges of jam! After dinner they had to amuse themselves in the playground or on the school fields in all weathers, but we could choose between playing in the garden, *Listen With Mother* on the wireless or a rest in the bedroom. 'A rest' reminds me of my brother, Mike, while 'a rest in the bedroom' recalls one particularly eventful lunchtime.

At the time of the following incident Mike hadn't yet started his struggle through the education system and was still at home with Mum, but Julie and I were let out of school at twelve o'clock as usual. Julie was in the Infants so she hadn't far to walk, but I was a Junior and had to use the school gateway furthest from our house. It only took a minute to run home but by the time I'd reached the back door Julie had already started her savoury mince and mashed potato.

'Get your brother, please,' was Mum's greeting before I had even tried to avoid washing my hands. 'I've called him twice. I don't know what he's doing up there.'

'There' was the sparsely furnished bedroom Mike and I shared. It contained one double bed, also shared; two chests of drawers – a tall one in which Mum kept blankets, sheets and towels, and a small one on Mike's side of the bed in which were kept some of our clothes; a bedside table and tiny reading lamp on my side of the bed; a green cane chair that Nana Pegg had given me as a christening present; the rug upon which at that very moment my brother was probably sitting, surrounded by a chaos of my comics.

'Do I have to?' I whined, desperate to catch up with Julie just in case there were seconds of savoury mince.

'Get your brother now,' Mum repeated firmly. 'And wash those hands in the bathroom. Properly. They're filthy.'

I stomped upstairs, banged a clenched fist on our bedroom door, shouted 'Dinner!' and went into the bathroom to run cold water over the tips of my fingers. As I did this I heard my brother slowly open and carefully close the bedroom door, and then charge downstairs with an urgency which indicated he'd suddenly remembered Julie's fondness for seconds of savoury mince.

When I eventually sat down at the table, having been ordered to wash my hands AGAIN, both Mike and Julie were being served second helpings. Mum put aside a little extra for me, but threatened to give it to the others if I stomped or banged once more.

The pattern of our lunchtime was fairly predictable and while we ate we used to do one of four things. We sometimes talked to each other; we regularly quarrelled, usually over the division of seconds; we often listened to *Workers' Playtime*; we always watched other children watching us. These other children were our fellow Ruislip Gardens pupils who liked to watch us eat, talk, quarrel or listen to the wireless. They stared at us through the fence which separated our garden from the school fields as if we were performers at the zoo, pointing and waving and laughing at our every gesture. Sometimes Mum went into the garden and politely asked them to go away, but more often a patrolling dinner lady wandered across and shepherded them elsewhere.

On this particular day, however, two dinner ladies stood amongst the staring children and seemed also to be waving and pointing at us. Julie and I waved back.

'I like those dinner ladies. Sometimes they do skipping with the girls,' my sister enthused.

'I wish they'd leave us in peace. Don't wave back and they might go away,' Mum moaned.

They didn't go away but looked to be adding shouting to their waving and pointing. We couldn't hear what they might have been shouting above the canteen noise of *Workers' Playtime* which crackled from our wireless, so Mum asked Julie to find out if they wanted something. Julie, though, hadn't finished her savoury mince and wasn't about to leave it for either of her brothers to pinch. I had finished mine – in record time without stomp or bang – and asked Mum for the promised seconds. 'See what they want while I get it, then,' she bargained, so I went into the garden, desperately restraining my frustration and a fierce desire to stomp and bang.

As soon as I got outside I heard what our audience had been shouting, I understood why they'd been waving and I saw what they'd been pointing at. They were shouting 'Fire!' and pointing up at my bedroom window. It was part-open and thick grey smoke billowed through it. I panicked. I waved at my mum, pointed at my bedroom and joined the chorus of 'Fire! Fire!' Mum and Julie ran into the garden and looked in horror at the smoke which continued to pour out and get blacker.

'Someone's phoned the fire brigade,' a dinner lady's voice attempted to reassure my ashen-faced mum.

85

'Would you like one of us to collect the children, Mrs Pegg, and look after them here?' offered another voice in the growing crowd.

'Yes, please. Thank you,' Mum replied in a sort of trance. She just stared at the smoke escaping through the bedroom window and repeated 'Yes, please. Thank you,' several times.

A dinner lady soon came to take Julie, Mike and me into school. We had hardly closed our garden gate behind us when ringing bells announced the imminent arrival of the Middlesex Fire Brigade in Stafford Road, and just as we walked through the main entrance to the school a fire engine halted outside our house, closely pursued by another. I stopped in the doorway, wanting to watch firemen leap into action, unreel their hoses and lean ladders against my house, but the firm hand of a dinner lady dragged me away. I suppose she was concerned about possible damaging psychological effects on three young minds, but I considered this most unfair. After all, it's not every day that you can watch your own home burned to the ground, is it? Furthermore, all the children in the school had been alerted to the incident and were at that very moment pressing up against the fence and squealing with excitement. I loudly shouted and stomped my objection to this treatment, so loudly that Mr Griffiths was sent for and I was made to spend the remainder of my lunchtime in his classroom. I had to wait until I was back with my own class in the afternoon before a million and thirty-seven shrill voices informed me that my house hadn't been reduced to a heap of smouldering rubble.

I had to wait until I got home to learn why my house still stood where I'd left it a few hours earlier. Although everywhere stank of smoke, the fire had been confined to my bedroom. In fact, the fire hadn't spread beyond the small chest of drawers on my brother's side of our bed. The firemen had discovered the seat of the fire within seconds of dousing the chest with water.

'Looks as if someone's been playing with matches, Mrs Pegg,' Mum was solemnly informed. 'Got any idea?'

She had a very good idea, but that would have landed her in a police station answering questions about my brother's disappearance.

'Michael,' she whispered with a sigh. 'Wait until his father gets home.'

It wasn't long before my brother's father arrived home on his motor cycle, and it didn't take him long to get a full confession, either.

Earlier that day, just as Julie started eating savoury mince and I was being told to wash my filthy hands, Mike hadn't been sitting in our bedroom untidying my comics. He'd been sitting in our bedroom testing how safe safety matches were. When I had banged on the door and shouted 'Dinner!' Mike had put the lighted match that was in his hand into the matchbox, and had then put the matchbox into the bottom drawer of the small chest. Luckily for my brother, Dad had made the chest from wood which he'd previously used in the construction of scenery for a show at 'Q'. All scenery has to be fireproofed. That chest was fireproofed. The house was reprieved. Not so the safety-match tester, though. After Dad had dealt with him I expect his bottom was redder than a fire engine.

The next day some council workmen came to help Mum clean up, and a little later they redecorated for us, but it was a long time before the smell of smoke completely disappeared from our house. It clung in the corners of the rooms, to the edges of rugs and the pages of my comics, to remind each of us about that day in different ways. Dad remembered the long, slow journey from Kew to Ruislip, all the time worrying what he might find at the top of Stafford Road. Mum recalled feeling sick as she stood hypnotized by the awful sight of smoke pouring from our bedroom. Julie laughed at the thought of us waving back at the dinner ladies. Mike probably . . . Well, who can tell what goes on inside my brother's head? Could that firm-handed dinner lady really have been serious about causing him psychological damage? And what of me? I might not remember the names of the dinner ladies or how many firemen leapt into action, or the colour of Mum's pinafore, or the number of times Dad whacked Mike, but I could never forget never getting seconds of savoury mince.

WINNIE THE POOH,
DO YOU LIKE ME?
AND WALLY MEDHURST

Although I liked some of my teachers, I never had much time for education. I hated schooldays, even when I was very tiny. I was the first child to escape from Ruislip Gardens Nursery School on three consecutive days, thereby forcing the headmistress to lock and bolt the entrance gate and strap me into my canvas bed for the compulsory afternoon rest. At the infants' school I kicked another headmistress, Miss Allcock, on the shin as she told me off in a music lesson in the hall. I'm not sure if I was reacting to the public reprimand, Miss Allcock's piano style or 'Authority', but I never improved as I moved through the education system, majoring in Conflict Studies almost everywhere I went.

At my junior school there were several teachers whose wrath I found easy to incur. Most notable of these was Mr Baum, fiery-tempered and slipper-wielding Mr Baum who still plays occasional cameo roles in my nightmares, his large nose made even larger and his snarling menace made more menacing by the distortions of time. Mr Baum lashed out with tongue and size nine slipper in all directions, but mainly mine and Philip Axtell's. I was slippered regularly – about once a week, I suppose – but Philip got the slipper VERY regularly – just about once a day. I'm not exaggerating the extent of his punishment, the days when he didn't get beaten being memorably rare. We were both slippered for typical schoolboy misdemeanours such as spilling ink, not paying attention, answering back, talking in assembly, whispering in class and shouting in the corridor.

No other teacher punished minor misdeeds as frequently or ferociously as Mr Baum, a man in a class of his own when it came to making miserable the lives of schoolchildren. He seemed to get the greatest pleasure from picking on the most disadvantaged boys, like Philip, whose untidy red hair and freckled face marked him out as an obvious target in even the most crowded classroom.

Another boy, Winston Pugh, angered Mr Baum even more than Philip or I did, getting literally right up our teacher's nose. 'Winnie the Pooh' was Winston's nickname, and without going into details I can honestly state that in all my schooldays I never encountered a more appropriate one. Winston's mother may have been patriotic and proudly Conservative, but she wasn't very particular over personal hygiene. Mr Baum would definitely have agreed with me, and he let her unfortunate son know just how great a nasal irritant he was every single time that Winston queued to have his work marked. Children can be just as cruel as teachers, and sometimes those of us who were already queuing returned to our desks when Winston joined the line. On these occasions, Mr Baum could be observed holding his breath while rapidly ticking the offending boy's book, regardless of whether it was right or wrong, ticks being quicker to execute than crosses. However, when we kept our places and let Winston stand behind us – only someone with a heavy cold or a poor memory would stand behind Winston – you could watch Mr Baum grow crosser as the queue shrank. And as Winston got nearer, Mr Baum's nostrils flared wider and his sensitive nose grew redder, its owner inwardly seething and steaming, Etna on the edge of eruption. By the time of their inevitable collision beside Mr Baum's chair and right beneath his nose, the rest of us were crouched and waiting

in silence
in fear
in pairs
in desks
in rows

in anticipation of the imminent explosion. Winston nervously rubbed his rolled-up exercise book against his backside while Mr Baum slowly looked him down and up; peered down at dirty, flimsy basketball boots; sneered at grey socks fallen round grimy ankles; stared at bruised and unwashed knees; glared at unbuttoned flies; drifted his gaze from loose and useless braces to sleeveless grey pullover, pulled down but not down enough to hide the holes in a woollen vest; surveyed the neck and nose of a coalman. The rolled-up exercise book rose up to rub the neck as the nose sniffed up two long sniffs; Mr Baum stood up, looked down his own enormous nose at Winston's matted hair, and exploded.

!
!
!
'You
are a
dirty &
smellypig
it's always
one big stink
in this room at
the end of each &
everyday/tell me do
you ever wash in your
house? do you never have

soap at home? I bet you've
not seen soap and water for
weeks you dirty little smelly
little boy/I refuse to mark any
more of your books until you stop
coming to school smelling like that
and change your habits your pants and
socks/get out and stay out/understand?'

Mr Baum was my second-year teacher at junior school, succeeded for almost all of my final two years by Miss Astell. She was not as fiery as Mr Baum but so unpredictable that life in her classroom was just like being in a pantomime directed by Alfred Hitchcock, with Miss Astell playing Dame, Giant, Ship's Cat, Wicked Queen, Fairy Godmother and both ends of the Horse, in addition to her favourite role of Shadow Behind The Shower Curtain. The knife-edge life experienced by the members of her company meant we never learned our cues, none of us certain when we should laugh or when it was wise to remain silent and solemn.

If I'd been a less able pupil I might have stayed a speechless extra in a crowd scene, just like the children who sat in convenient quiet on a 'slow table', the best days of their lives rarely troubled by any of the repertory villains I played opposite. However, being one of the most vociferous in the class – beside being nonconformist, cynical and cheeky – I often co-starred in Miss Astell's dramatic vignettes.

I was moved to a slow table only once, after an episode which illustrates perfectly the relationship Miss Astell and I endured. One of our teacher's stranger habits was incessantly to ask everyone in her class, 'You do like me, don't you?'

Everyone, even me, affirmed we liked her – anything for the quiet life, a life without the Wicked Queen and the Shadow. However, in our first summer term together I tired of this facile dialogue and threw some spontaneous anarchy into one of Miss Astell's harmless little mannered encounters.

'You do like me, don't you?' she asked me for the millionth time that week, as she patrolled the room and I struggled to master long division.

'No, I don't like you!' I shouted. 'I don't like you and I've never liked you. In fact, I hate you.'

Miss Astell stood open-mouthed and dumbfounded, as open-mouthed and dumb as if she'd found Mr Baum dancing naked on a table in the staff room. Everyone else stopped living, statues save for eyes which zapped between my outburst and Miss Astell's response.

'What did you say?'

'I don't like you,' I confirmed. 'I'm fed up with the same stupid question. I don't like you any more.'

Miss Astell must have been wounded by my barbed remarks, I'm sure, but a wounded Miss Astell was a woman at her most unpredictable and dangerous.

'After all I've done for you,' she counter-attacked. 'Is this the thanks I get in return?'

She then directed her pleas to the spectating class, she anxious for their sympathy and the class anxious for me to remain her only target.

'Is this not the boy to whom I always give extra spellings whenever he asks for them?'

A few heads nodded.

'Is this not the boy to whom I loaned my very own personal copy of *The Observer Book of Pond Life*?'

Most heads nodded.

'Is this not the same boy to whom I entrusted the care of Our Class Nature Table?'

My head was the only abstention.

'Well, Stephen Pegg, if this is the way that you treat all of us there will be no more privileges for you. Starting from now, you can take your things and move from this table. These nice children don't want you spoiling their group, do you?'

Divide and rule. Every head shook obediently. That was how I lost the prestigious Nature Table job and was relegated to a 'slow table' for a few weeks.

Miss Astell continued to ask the other children if they liked her or not, especially at the end of the Christmas term. During the season of peace, goodwill, nativity plays, paper chains and class parties, she expected to receive a present from each of her pupils. During December she bombarded us with hints about Christmas and gifts, aiming with such precision that even I, in the final week of term, reluctantly joined a procession of children for the gift-giving ceremony. If this had merely meant handing over the bath cubes or box of Meltis Fruits, or whatever my mum had bought and wrapped, I might not have loathed the occasion quite so much. Unfortunately, after each of us had given Miss Astell her present she liked to feign surprise, unwrap, demand, 'You do like me, don't you?' and kiss the unlucky gift-giver an enormous slobbery smacker on the cheek.

I somehow endured this traumatic experience but other children often fled in terror from Miss Astell's embrace. This never saved them from a fate worse than tests, though, the Christmas-crazed spinster pursuing them around the room until they had been trapped by other children and forcibly rewarded. Some of my classmates were psychologically damaged for life, I'm sure. Indeed, Victor Holden, who was once dragged kicking from under Our Nature Table following a Grand National of a chase, never married. I imagine that every time he went to kiss a girl, and every time a girl went to kiss him, the ghost of Miss Astell pounced to slobber all over his libido.

'Thank you, Victor. You do really like me after all, don't you?'

Apart from my short vacation on a 'slow table', I was one of the chosen few who received special tuition from Miss Astell. I didn't particularly want her extra help, but she was determined to dispense it so that as many of her pupils as possible passed the eleven plus examination. However, while she wanted us to be compliant and conscientious, I sought only to enjoy myself and make others laugh. The inevitable outcome of this clash of wills was continuous conflict.

Miss Astell never bashed with the enthusiasm of Mr Baum, but frequently punished me with pages of pointless line-writing or lengthy periods of solitary sentry duty outside the classroom door. I always enjoyed the latter, just so long as Mr Croft, the headmaster, didn't come creeping along the corridor in brown suit and avuncular mood.

'Oh dear, oh dear. Stephen Pegg outside again. What have we been up to this time? Let's pop in and see what Miss Astell has to say about you.'

Miss Astell always had plenty to say about me, much of it irritatingly true. After she'd catalogued my most recent misdemeanours for Mr Croft, I would have to return to my place, sit down and start working once again. Alone. In silence. The others were allowed to tidy away their books, put down gently their sleepy heads on cool, grainy desk lids, switch their brains to daydream mode and prepare for Miss Astell to read them the next instalment of her alter ego's history, *The Adventures of Toad of Toad Hall*.

Miss Astell, like Mr Toad, was nothing if not persuasive. She was eccentric, it's true, and egocentric, too, but she did persuade me to work hard enough to become one of eight who passed that divisive eleven-plus exam and went to a grammar school.

$$11+11+11+11+11+11+11$$

Most of the other children in Ruislip Gardens' fourth year left to have their education furthered at Manor Secondary Modern, while a few went to Bourne or Queensmead Secondary Mods. For a long time I didn't realize that 'secondary' referred to a stage in the education system and equated secondary with second-rate. Even the briefest comparison of their buildings and facilities not only served to reinforce my misunderstanding but also highlighted the unfairness of the eleven-plus selection system. While children who failed the examination were made to feel inferior, all sorts of adults constantly told me to make the most of the superior 'Grammar School Education' which I'd been fortunate enough to obtain.

At the time I didn't much care about taking advantage of an educational opportunity. I only knew that going to grammar school altered forever many friendships, some of them going back to nursery days. The same boys with whom I'd played cricket round Bromley Park in the August of 1959 had become near-strangers by the following October. I queued for buses, ran for trains and travelled for ages as they walked and cycled to their nearby schools; while I struggled with homework every weekday evening, they started going to youth clubs; on Saturday mornings, when they got jobs and earned money, I got cold, wet, muddy and miserable in school rugby matches. I envied my friends' freedom from uniform and petty rules; I longed to hang around the chip shop with them until after nine, to chat up girls and be reckless on a track bike with no lights. I don't suppose they envied much about my elevation to Ickenham and the grammar school. They probably watched me trudge up Stafford Road each evening, weighed down by a brown leather satchel and parental expectations, and told themselves:

'Grammar school! Blimey, if that's what it does to you, stuff that for a lark!'

My first day at grammar school set the tone for the next eight years when I arrived late and met the headmaster for a memorable but brief encounter. Vyners School was

Walking to Ickenham
with Julie on a Sunday
afternoon in 1951

My first Durham
summer, boating on
the Wear with Dad
in 1954

One of those school photographs, taken before a milk break in 1955

Jelly without eels in 'Q' Theatre after watching the pantomime in 1955

Grammar-school boy posing as enigmatic youth in 1961

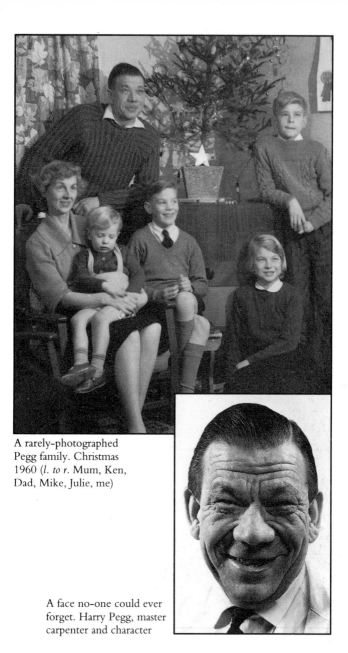

A rarely-photographed
Pegg family. Christmas
1960 (*l. to r.* Mum, Ken,
Dad, Mike, Julie, me)

A face no-one could ever
forget. Harry Pegg, master
carpenter and character

Look what happened when I followed the chocolate cake to Backwell. 14 July 1973 (*photograph Brian Tolhurst*)

Teaching at Birdwell School, near Bristol, in 1978

Well, was it really
April 1984?
Seems like only
dreams away

Eleanor's first
shoes didn't
need a stretching
machine. May
1984

Water baby photographed in 1984 (for purpose of embarrassing daughter in front of future boyfriends)

Happy family, even though Ros and I knew that MND was progressing relentlessly. November 1987 (*photograph Derek Hibbert*)

Giant strides in Cornwall, just days after diagnosis. May 1987

Portscatho
holiday.
August 1986

Storytime, January 1986

Still a happy family, despite lost teeth. April 1990 (*photograph Woman*)

Resident writer, April 1990

Twinkling twinkling, little star of Channel 4 film *Just Some Stories For Eleanor* with the writer. February 1990 (*photograph Neil Turner, Insight*)

still being built in September 1959 so for one term all the first-year pupils were taught (by Vyners teachers) at St Mary's Grammar School for Girls in Eastcote.

The day before term began my dad drove me to the bus terminus in Ruislip where we saw a route 158 double decker that showed Eastcote Lane on its destination indicator. Dad asked a bus inspector if the 158 went to Eastcote Lane and, of course, the inspector said 'Yes', although he didn't know which was the stop for St Mary's.

'The conductor will be able to tell you that,' he suggested, and that was good enough for Dad and me.

Next morning I rose early, washed and dressed, breakfasted, was wished well and driven to Ruislip. Armed with brand new satchel and London Transport bus pass, I climbed to the top deck of a near-empty 158 and sat in my favoured back seat. I wasn't at all alarmed by the absence of other Vyners uniforms because I knew that it was early. Furthermore, I intended to make a good impression by being one of the first to arrive at St Mary's. The conductor said he'd tell me when we reached the school in Eastcote Lane so I sat back to enjoy the journey.

I only enjoyed the first five minutes, those twin impostors Anxiety and Apprehension climbing the stairs and squeezing in either side of me immediately after the bus had turned right at Ruislip Manor traffic lights instead of proceeding straight ahead towards Eastcote. In another ten minutes, at South Ruislip, I was nearer home than I had been half an hour earlier and beginning to suspect that perhaps I hadn't chosen the most direct route to St Mary's. However, somewhere near South Harrow the bus conductor shouted up the stairs, 'Here's your school, son.' It wasn't. It wasn't a grammar school. It wasn't a girls' school. And what's more, it wasn't anywhere near Eastcote. 'This is Eastcote Lane, son,' said the conductor as he examined my bus pass. 'You want Fore Street in

Eastcote. That's not on this route. You'd better go back to Ruislip and ask an inspector what bus you want.'

Almost an hour later I was back at the Ruislip terminus, complaining to myself that you can never find a bus inspector when you really need one. Eventually one arrived, casually alighting from a 204 as if I had all day to reach my destination; casually in the way that all bus inspectors alight from a moving bus as it slows or rounds a corner; casually with black raincoat flapping behind, a crow about to swoop upon a carcass in a field.

Picking through the bones of my story and flicking through the pages of his pocket timetable, Inspector Crow informed me that a 98b would get me to Fore Street but warned that my bus pass only entitled me to travel free before ten o'clock. As it was half-past nine I thought I had plenty of time before my pass expired, but the inspector preened his raincoat and squawked that the next 98b was timetabled to leave at 10.01. I protested that I had no money, only a cheque for half a term's school dinners. Crow slowly turned the flimsy pages of his timetable, searching deliberately, carefully, oh so slowly until, with the rapidity of his cousin the woodpecker, he told me, 'Quick – 9.36 – 98a – High Street stop – by the chip shop – off you go.' And off I flew, leaving him to strut menacingly around the terminus in pursuit of other victims, an unsuspecting tardy driver, perhaps, or innocent novice conductress.

{98a}{98a}{98a}{98a}

When I walked through the gates and across the empty playground of St Mary's it was well past ten o'clock and I was wishing that I'd made the shorter journey to Manor Secondary Modern School with most of my friends. As the heads of hundreds of grammar-school girls swung round to observe me wish my way across their playground, my own head bent down to watch my size seven sensible shoes carry me away from their stares and whispers.

I was still wishing I was somewhere else when I met my headmaster, Mr Jagger, the black gown that billowed behind him reminding me of the bird I had so recently encountered. While I told him about my excursion to South Harrow he craned his neck in all directions, surveying the corridor for something more suited to his status than a lost child. Unable to find anything or anyone else, he stopped me from leaping onto that 98a near the chip shop and escorted me to my classroom. Knocking at the door and entering the room simultaneously, he waited only long enough for teacher and pupils to rise from their chairs before announcing with a hint of derision, 'This is Stephen Pegg, Miss Naylor. He caught the wrong bus.'

Mr Jagger leered triumphantly. Miss Naylor smiled sympathetically. Miss Naylor's class laughed nervously.

'Now where shall I put him?' he asked. 'Here's a space next to Penelope Atcheler,' he answered.

'Not a girl!' I protested, but Mr Jagger was off and out of the room before Penelope had countered, 'Not a boy!'

Many elements contributed to the conflicts of my schooldays – uniforms, reports, rules, examinations, teachers, homework, headmasters and headmistresses – but I must admit that my attitude played an important part. At primary school I was competitive, cynical, too clever by half, and at grammar school I was lazy and flippant but not clever enough. At both schools I hated having to conform to regulations and adult expectations, but most of all I hated work. Schoolwork, that is. I never minded any sort of work for which I was paid, only appreciating the intrinsic rewards that can be won from academic effort when I was at college in the early seventies.

I suppose that my interest in working for financial

reward dates back to when I was ten and my pocket money amounted to a meagre 10d a week, just one old penny for each candle on my last birthday cake. Even in 1958 that didn't buy many sweets or comics so I went in search of additional income. My first jobs were confined to weekends and holidays but by the time I was sixteen I was a regular midweek worker, helping out at the Piccadilly Theatre whenever Dad was short of showmen. The work was interesting and well-paid but time-consuming and tiring, sometimes keeping me out of my bed until after midnight. Such distractions obviously contributed to my lack of academic success, although my various work experiences taught me to be adaptable and resourceful, and built my self-confidence in a way that no amount of successfully completed home-work assignments or glowing school reports could ever have done. Anyway, that's how I justify my pursuit of pounds, shillings and pence.

All children are influenced by things that adults do and say. I must have been greatly impressed by my father's desire to increase the size of his wage packet by working many hours of overtime. When I compared our circumstances to most of my friends', our car, clothes and regular holidays confirmed relative affluence. It also seemed to me that my dad was treated as something of a celebrity whenever I went anywhere with him. I must have equated his fame and fortune with hard work, and therefore sought to emulate him through paid employ-ment rather than academic success.

At about this time I also heard my dad say something which further served to reinforce my educational preju-dice. He was telling my Uncle Bill about an Oxbridge graduate who was working with him at 'Q' Theatre, scathingly observing, 'All that education – first class honours degree in something or other – and the useless bastard doesn't know how to use a Yankee screwdriver.' Well, that gave me an additional excuse for not working hard at school and I henceforth directed my energy and enthusiasm elsewhere.

My earliest jobs were either unpaid or undertaken in exchange for pocket money, ordinary tasks like washing up after meals or going to the shops. I didn't especially enjoy household chores, probably because I had to do them with Julie and Mike, but I was always pleased to escape from my brother and sister by going to the shops in New Pond Parade. My very first shopping errand was not unlike the picture book *Don't forget the bacon!* by Pat Hutchins. The little boy in her story eventually remembered all the things that he'd been sent to buy, except for the bacon. I had only two items to remember – a half-pound of butter and three pounds of potatoes – but still returned home with an empty shopping bag. Mum hadn't given me a note, confident that her bright little six-year-old would remember what he'd been sent to buy. Unfortunately, by the time I had reached the shops I wasn't sure whether I should ask for half a pound of potatoes and three pounds of butter or three pounds of potatoes and half a pound of butter.

Eventually, like the boy who forgot the bacon, I set off for the shops once again, this time clutching a hastily-scribbled note. In Frank Norman I bought half a pound of New Zealand butter and from George, the greengrocer, I bought three pounds of English potatoes. But not before George had confused me with his favourite joke.

'Do you want King Edward's? Just tell the lazy old devil to fetch his own, next time!'

While Julie, Mike and I were small, Mum used to leave an order at Frank Norman during the week and on Friday evening a delivery boy would arrive on our front doorstep with a box of surprises. I was surprised by what Mum had ordered, and she was surprised by what turned up. Almost every Friday an inquest was held in our kitchen, Mum declaring, 'I'm sure I never ordered that,' as an excited Julie and I unpacked the box. And almost every Saturday morning, after breakfast and *Children's Favourites*, we walked down to the shops and listened to an explanation from a man in Frank Norman:

'I'm sorry, Mrs Pegg, no Scotts Oats. That's why I sent you Quaker instead.'

'You ordered mild Cheddar, Mrs Pegg? We've only got the Canadian.'

'Too streaky, Mrs Pegg? It's what I normally send you, but I'll change it if you want.'

'I'm sorry, Mrs Pegg. I thought I'd popped a blue bag in with your order. Can't wash on Monday without the old blue bag, can we?'

The boy from Frank Norman wasn't the only person to call at our front door with something to sell or deliver. The milkman called, of course, but every day of the week then. Furthermore, up until about 1956 the milkman's float was horse-drawn. The Express Dairy horse was a huge, plodding, chestnut creature which always had its head in a nosebag when it stopped near our house. As it moved off down Stafford Road it inevitably left a trail of steaming turds which Julie and I were encouraged to collect by Mum and Dad. These horse droppings, we were regularly reminded, were reputed to be 'good for the rhubarb'. As far as I could tell, it made no difference whatsoever, and rhubarb was only improved when extra sugar was added to the custard.

Two milkmen competed for customers in Ruislip Gardens, the Express Dairy man and one from the London Cooperative Society. Mum floated from one to the other for years, changing allegiance as often as she felt she was being overcharged. We also had two bakers delivering bread when we first lived on our estate. I sometimes helped the Prices' man, very occasionally earning myself half a crown although I was quite content just to ride in his electric van and be rewarded with a couple of cakes. The delivery man had his round – those homes he regularly called at – and he carried bread from door to door in a large wicker basket. His customers selected a loaf, if they wanted one, and paid for it there and then. Sometimes I drove the van, and I often accompanied the baker to front doors, but I mostly kept the back of the van tidy, sweeping breadcrumbs from the floor and out onto the road for the birds. I suppose that the baker made a living from his round while many of the Ruislip Gardens mothers were tied to their homes by the demands of tiny children, but as families grew up and shopping trips became easier his days were numbered. Eventually the baker's roundsman, just like the horse-drawn milk float, disappeared from our lives.

When the three Pegg children became a little more manageable, Mum ventured as far as Ruislip and Ruislip Manor to do her shopping. On the return journey she wearily pushed an enormous black pram which contained Julie, Mike and assorted groceries. I walked in front of the pram with my head in a comic, expecting Mum to shout a warning whenever I was about to collide with a tree or post or oncoming pedestrian. Inevitably, though, the pram was not successfully containing Julie, Mike or groceries and Mum was struggling to contain her temper, so the first I knew about an imminent collision was the collision itself. If I'd had a penny for every time I apologized to a tree or post or oncoming pedestrian, I might never have needed to supplement my pocket money.

Between 1954 and 1973 I walked, whistled, ran, sang, hopped, hurried, scooted, skated, skipped, tripped, tricycled and bicycled to one or other of the shops in New Pond Parade hundreds of times. None were self-service shops until the mid sixties so I also learned how to queue. Patiently. Sometimes I queued too patiently, I recall, since I seemed to be forever encountering grown-ups who ignored the queuing convention whenever small children waited in front of them.

I was most often the victim of queue-jumpers in the baker's and the sweet shop. When I got fed up with this mistreatment and indignantly asserted my tiny self, the grown-ups inevitably feigned surprise and fibbed. The usual fib in either of the bakers was 'Sorry son, never saw you there,' whilst the pick of the sweet shop selection was 'I thought you were still making up your mind.'

There were two sweet shops in New Pond Parade, Bunces and Bradshaws. To get to Bunces I had to cross the busy West End Road, a hazardous undertaking even in those days, so I shopped in Bradshaws whenever possible. Mum often sent me there for a *Daily Sketch* and five Weights – that tabloid newspaper because she considered it superior to the *Daily Mirror* that most of our neighbours read, and five cigarettes because that was probably all she could afford to deduct from her housekeeping money.

Bradshaws was once run by an ex-professional foot-baller who claimed he'd played at Preston North End with Tommy Docherty. We often used to talk about football, and I can still remember him describing the nastier characteristics of The Doc after his transfer from Preston to Arsenal. Years later, when Tommy Docherty lost his job as manager of Chelsea, I recalled the inside information I'd received in Bradshaws and sagely told myself that his fall from grace was inevitable.

At the far end of Bradshaws was the post office counter where I cashed the half-crown postal orders sent to me by my grandmothers each January. Nana Foster and Nana Pegg must have foreseen my literary career and always selected a birthday card containing some memorable lines of sentimental verse:

> To my darling grandson
> On this very extra special day,
> Hoping you have lots of splendid fun
> With all your friends both bright and gay.

I also bought postal orders here, for Mum to send off

to Liverpool each week with her ten-crossed coupon and dreams of a small fortune. Not a large fortune but a 'just enough to' sum: just enough to be able to sail to Australia and visit her brother; just enough to buy a new Rolls Razor twin-tub washing machine; just enough to move to a detached house in Grosvenor Vale; and just enough to send me down the road to Bradshaws for twenty cigarettes instead of only five. Every Saturday evening Mum checked her copy coupon, either by listening to the radio or looking in the *Standard*, which someone sold door-to-door on Saturdays during the football season. And every Saturday evening Mum's mixture of birthday numbers and uninformed guesses failed to alter our lives, her 'just enough to' dreams replaced by 'if only' regrets.

At the post office counter I occasionally bought a National Savings stamp, always a one-shilling stamp with a portrait of Princess Anne looking uncannily like Julie aged six. I could never afford to invest half a crown in a stamp which featured Prince Charles and one of his ears sitting in a kilt and staring at some distant event, doubtless dreaming of growing up to be an architect.

Those savings stamps wouldn't be very popular today. Firstly, they earned no interest, so no self-respecting Thatcher investorette would put money into such a venture. Secondly, the stamps were flagrantly sexist in the way they were valued, and must have helped to damage the perception of their relative worth of millions of little girls and boys. They certainly seemed to harm Princess Anne's self-esteem. When she was going through her surly, sulky, unloved phase in the late sixties and early seventies, I'm sure that she was reacting against all those years when she'd been the cheaper National Savings stamp. And why does she now work so tirelessly on behalf of the Save The Children Fund? Perhaps she wants to pay back all those children who had once saved her.

Next door to Bradshaws was West End Fisheries, where I often bought bags of chips, occasionally treated myself to fish and chips and was sometimes sent to buy wet fish which Mum cooked at home. During the day it was an open-fronted shop without doors, made secure at night by heavy shutters. Inside the shop were three sloping white-tiled display counters, separated by two gangways which led to the rear where the frying was done. Every day, excluding Sundays and Mondays, wet fish and shellfish were displayed: shoals of herring swimming with an armada of burnished kippers; colonies of shrimps clustered next to a fleet of filleted cod; a fearsome crab poised to climb into a pool of sprats; golden haddock diving into a bed of parsley. Some of those fish used to watch me as I stood in the queue for lunchtime chips; and they always stared at me reproachfully whenever I sidled past with a freshly-cooked cousin wrapped in newspaper and destined for my dad's dinner plate.

This fishy tale is, of course, entirely trawled up from the depths of my imagination. In reality, most fish was left in the boxes in which it arrived from Billingsgate, remaining on view until about four o'clock when the sloping counters were cleared, scrubbed and hosed down, the unsold fish dispatched to a cold store or dropped in a dustbin. Most of it, I suspect, ended up in the dustbin, for people didn't buy wet fish as often as they do today. Mum, for instance, only bought fish on Fridays, a Catholic tradition learned from Nana Foster and kept by Mum despite her claim to be 'lapsed'. We also occasionally ate grilled roe on toast for tea on Saturdays, but the owner of West End Fisheries was never going to make his fortune while families like mine bought fish so rarely, and the business was sold in about 1961 to a man named Savvides. He stopped selling wet fish, removed the sloping white-tiled display counters, had a glass shopfront installed, put in Formica-topped tables and vinyl-covered chairs, put up the prices and sold only fish and chips. And fishcake and chips. And pie and chips, pasty and chips, saveloy and chips, chips and chips . . .

In January 1961, after I'd pleaded with him for months, Dad bought me a racing bike for my birthday. It was a red Claud Butler with five Campagnolo gears and a Renold's 531 frame, cost £26 and was bought from Curry's in Ruislip. For a while I wasn't allowed to cycle to school, but once I had convinced Dad that I could steer safely with drop handlebars I swapped bus queues and train journeys for cycle races.

For three years I used to sprint up West End Road with Brian Bardrick and Alan Franklin, two of my first friends at Vyners. Most mornings I waved to David Barker, a 'lost' friend from junior school days, as he cycled in the opposite direction. David was rushing home to change into his school clothes and snatch a second breakfast, having just delivered newspapers to almost a hundred Ruislip homes. I knew this because I'd once been a paperboy with David.

No sooner had I gratefully received my racing bike than I wanted to have the appropriate accessories, things like fingerless cycle gloves and 'rat traps' for the pedals. These all cost money, much more money than I possessed, so I urgently needed a part-time job. David had suggested that a paper round for W. H. Smith, where he'd worked since leaving Ruislip Gardens Juniors, was an easy way of earning money. So easy, in fact, that he did two rounds before school each morning.

One Saturday afternoon in April 1961 David and I had cycled to Smith's in Ruislip where I was introduced to the shop manager. He briefly explained what I would have to do and asked if I could start on Monday. Anxious to get my feet into rat traps and my hands inside a pair of fingerless cycle gloves, I answered 'Yes, please,' and the job was mine for 10/6d (52p) a week.

The following Monday I woke before six, at least an

hour earlier than usual, yawned a protest at the alarm clock and shivered my way to the bathroom. Mum was already up and cooking, the aroma of frying bacon and tomatoes robustly climbing the stairs as I drifted sleepily in the opposite direction. After breakfast I carefully wheeled my Claud Butler out of the shed, strapped my rolled-up yellow cape to the back of my saddle and pedalled off down Stafford Road to rendezvous with David at his front garden.

At W. H. Smith my fifty-two newspapers had already been marked. I loaded them into my bag and set out in search of my territory. Ten minutes later I was back at the shop, offloading half my papers because I'd found it so difficult to cycle with a full bag. The newspaper readers of my territory favoured the weightier journals such as *The Times* and *Telegraph* whereas both David's rounds comprised mainly tabloids like the *Sketch* and *Mirror*. No wonder he was able to do two rounds before school.

By the time I'd finished my round, having earlier gone back to the shop to collect the rest of my papers, it was almost half-past eight. At this time I would normally be somewhere between West Ruislip station and Ickenham pond, furiously racing to school to copy maths homework answers from Phil Yates or Roger Collard. By the time I'd cycled home and exchanged my scruffy kickabout clothes for Vyners uniform it was ten to nine, a time when I would normally be somewhere between clever boys in the playground. That day I didn't get to school until half-past nine, too late for copying but late enough to cop a detention. Next morning things went a little better, and each succeeding morning I became more efficient. By Friday I even reached the playground in time to compare my physics homework with Roger Collard's and make a few crucial alterations.

The following week, though, it rained every day. It seemed to rain most heavily between seven and eight, soaking my shoes and corduroy trousers, rivuleting down my neck, ruining the breakfast table reading of fifty-two Ruislip residents. By the end of that week I'd had enough of early alarm calls, cold bathrooms, wet clothes, detentions for being late and poor marks for homework. I thanked David for suggesting a paper round but confessed that I'd rather go without fingerless cycle gloves and rat traps than repeat the experience of the previous fortnight. I thanked the manager of W. H. Smith for putting up with me, accepted my 10/6d, and cycled into Ruislip High Street in search of easier employment.

David and I remained friends, although not especially close, until he and his parents moved to Cornwall in 1963. Four or five years later I heard he'd been killed by a hit-and-run driver as he walked along a narrow country lane with his girlfriend.

Some months after my unsuccessful attempt at being a paper boy, I got my first proper part-time job, in the Home & Colonial supermarket in Ruislip High Street. I was still thirteen, an age when the only out-of-school work that Vyners boys and girls were supposed to do was homework. Unfortunately for me, the school's senior mistress, Miss Holmes, shopped at Home & Colonial, so whenever I spied with my little eye a shopper beginning with H, I had to stop whatever I was doing and disappear into the stockroom until she'd left. Fortunately, though, the manager, Mr Brackley, didn't object to this, probably because he knew I was too young to be working there. He had given me the job as a favour to my dad, very likely an 'on the square' sort of favour which had been settled with a secret handshake between double Scotches in a saloon bar after a midweek Lodge meeting.

Mr Brackley was a busy man, always on the move as if afraid he'd be turned to a stack of two-pound bags of sugar if he ever stood still. His working life was spent rushing around from office >>> to >>> bacon counter >>> to >ʃ>ʃ> bank >>> to office

<<< out the back to <<< delivery bay >>> and on to >>> checkouts > cheese wrapping > shelf stacking >>> and finally to the staff room to see who was drinking tea when they really ought to have been rushing around like him.

Most of the shop assistants were married women, forever gossiping, laughing or teasing me. Mr Brackley referred to them collectively as 'the part-time ladies', a term of no endearment which tickled the cynic in me. I imagined that their hours away from stacking shelves and wrapping cheese were spent getting drunk, beating their children, spitting in public and swearing at the neighbours. The ladies, of course, did nothing worse than mildly curse the manager, always quietly and strictly on a part-time basis.

Mrs Brackley was one of the few full-time lady workers. The manager's wife was a couple of years younger than him but several dress sizes larger, a veritable Mrs Spratt to his lean Jack. She was in charge of the checkouts, and spent most of her day squeezed behind one of the tills where she could supervise the other cashiers.

Most of my work was done far from the cashiers and the formidable Mrs Spratt. I worked out the back, amongst the cardboard, the dustbins and the rats. Yes, rats. But first the cardboard. You get lots of cardboard in supermarkets since almost everything arrives in cardboard boxes, from washing powder to packet soup, sauce bottles to breakfast cereals. These boxes were unloaded by lorry drivers in the delivery bay at the rear of the supermarket. From there I carried them into the stockroom, where I stacked them tidily, or took them straight into the shop so the ladies could restock the shelves. When the boxes had been emptied they were taken to the rear of the store and thrown untidily on the ground. It was one of my jobs to create order out of the daily mess which accumulated here.

I didn't work alone. I had the rats for company. And

Wally Medhurst. Wally was 'the lad', the sort of young man that almost every shop used to employ to do the messy, menial tasks that no-one else would do for a next-to-nothing weekly wage. I know that I also did those tasks, but only at weekends, and I didn't face the prospect of a lifetime of poorly-paid messy, menial jobs. Wally was sixteen and had been at the Home & Colonial since leaving school; Wally was still waiting for a small wage rise; Wally had no ambition other than to own a motorbike; Wally was very tall but not very bright; Wally had enormous feet which he kept in enormous crepe-soled boots; Wally had an absent dad and incident-packed life. A few of Wally's Home & Colonial incidents involved me.

One of these occurred on a Saturday evening when Wally and I had arranged to have something to eat at his house before going to the pictures in Ruislip. We needed to get away from the shop as soon after closing time as possible so we'd already tidied the back yard and stockroom. On a normal Saturday we would then make sure that the shopping trolleys and baskets were stacked tidily, say good night and cycle home. This particular Saturday, however, Mr Brackley told us to clear the 'bacon counter' – a name not strictly accurate since cooked meats, cheese and a few other provisions were also sold from here. Most of these had to be moved to a cold store in the stockroom before the bacon counter was cleaned. Neither Wally nor I was too happy about enforced and unpaid overtime but we had no choice. Mr Brackley was a ruthless man who would have sacked us on the spot if we'd refused, so we cursed him under our breath and grudgingly began to remove trays of food.

After three or four journeys between the bacon counter and the stockroom I had resigned myself to missing the film at the Astoria. Since the main feature was about a gang of motorbike tearaways and an ex-speedway rider turned born-again Christian youth-club leader, I wasn't too downhearted. Wally, however, was livid. He'd talked about nothing other than motorbikes and speedway riders all day, and now it looked as if he would have to miss the film which some of his motorbike-mad friends had already seen every night that week. On our last journey to the stockroom Wally's mounting anger and disappointment finally turned him from 'the lad' to born-again tearaway. Snatching a boomerang-shaped liver sausage link from the white plastic tray I was carrying, Wally crouched in a baseball pitcher's pose, rose up, once again crouched down, wound himself up, sprang and flung that boomerang the length of the shop towards the stockroom door. Before I had time to gasp in horror it hit a ceiling fan and burst like a fragmentation bomb, splattering tiny bits of sausage all over the top of 'Breakfast Cereals' and the ceiling tiles above. Luckily for Wally, Mr Brackley was counting money by the checkouts, the sound of mixed silver drowning the manic laughter of the tearaway as he lay on his back, stamping his crepe soles on the floor and staring up at his handiwork.

With the last bacon joint and sausage link safely inside the cold store, Wally and I slipped away through the back door. At Wally's house we cooked ourselves tinned tomato soup, tinned steak and kidney pie with tinned processed peas, tinned carrots and chips, followed by tinned steamed pudding and evaporated milk. We ate this gourmet meal in Wally's front room while watching the telly. I don't remember what was on. We left the washing-up in the sink for Wally's mum.

As I've already said, it was my job to keep the cardboard tidy. I used to break up most of the boxes, flatten them and then stack them in piles ready for collection by the waste-paper man. Wally and I also used to burn cardboard, building huge towers from the corrugated inserts which came out of the boxes. When we set light to the bottom box, the inserts acted as a chimney and in next to no time our tower was burning as ferociously as any furnace. This practice was discouraged by Mr

Brackley, but Wally and I were potential pyromaniacs who found it hard to resist the roar of the flame and the smell of the smoke. We must have come close to destroying Ruislip High Street on several occasions, but the worst that actually happened was the loss of a rear tyre after Wally had left his track bike parked too near to the flames.

We weren't so lucky on another occasion when tidying cardboard, however. This incident occurred during the period when we were sharing the back yard with a large family of rats. They lived in a rubbish pile situated on the border between the Home & Colonial and Burtons (where, incidentally, I later bought my first suit). Wally sometimes used to park his track bike on this rubbish pile. Well, 'park' isn't really the correct word to describe the kamikaze way in which Wally leapt from the saddle of his still-speeding bike and allowed it to crash into whatever was in its path. Wally always managed to spot a perfect landing on his crepes, a huge grin of achievement underscoring his even huger nose as the bike toppled sideways. Wally's track bike was constructed entirely from parts he'd salvaged from bikes he'd previously wrecked, and it would, in time, be dismantled and cannibalized to create yet another potential wreck. Wally didn't care. He was only practising for the motorbike he longed to own.

The rats first appeared one Monday morning, two senior members of the family sitting on Wally's bike and enjoying a packet of stale Chiltonian custard creams stolen from a dustbin. The part-time lady who spotted them as she threw an empty box onto the cardboard mountain which Wally and I would shortly have to conquer, screamed and ran back inside the shop. By the time Mr Brackley came to investigate, the rats had dashed home to share out the remaining biscuits.

'Are you certain they were rats, and not large mice?' he questioned the part-time screamer.

113

'Of course I'm certain,' she shouted hysterically. 'I know a rat when I see one.'

The rodent exterminator was sent for, and Wally and I watched as he put gas pellets down every entrance and blocked every exit. Every entrance and exit except one, that is, the hole from which the rats would eventually emerge. After a while they duly appeared, dazed and disorientated, to be stunned by a blow on the neck and deposited in the exterminator's sack. One adult rat, however, managed to evade the exterminator and made a drunken meander for freedom. Wally chased it with an iron bar and smashed its skull at least ten times, just to make sure, he explained, it never again ate a picnic lunch on his track bike uninvited.

Within a fortnight the rats were back. Not those who'd been exterminated, and certainly not the one who'd been Wallyed, but some relatives who had been sent details of a 'desirable residence; close to shops; vacant possession'. It was a half-term Thursday afternoon, and I was working in the back yard. There had been a delivery half an hour earlier and Wally was moving boxes from the loading bay to the stockroom. A Man from Head Office had arrived unexpectedly and was inspecting the shop. Mr Brackley, in an attempt to grovel, ordered me to stop sweeping near the dustbins and wash the visitor's car. I dropped my brush and went into the staff room where I found a plastic bucket to fill with hot water. As I squirted some Squezy into the bucket, two part-time ladies interrupted their gossip about the Royal Family for a quick chorus of 'It's easy with Squezy, the washing-up wizard'. They laughed at their own spontaneity before turning on Princess Margaret.

'What you up to?' Wally asked as I struggled past him, soapy water slopping over my feet and the stockroom floor.

'Got to wash that Ford Zephyr out there. Seen it? Latest model, I think. Great, isn't it?'

He wasn't impressed. 'Rather have a Norton 650 any day.'

I left him dreaming of racing on the Isle of Man and lugging Echo margarine, Wally Medhurst – The Eastcote Greaser.

I got outside, put my bucket down on the loading bay and admired the car. Although I was still at an age when cycles and cycling preoccupied me, I could, nevertheless, appreciate the Zephyr's gleaming chrome and up-to-the-minute American styling. I was somewhere in mid-America when a noise from the dustbins distracted me. I looked across to my right, to where I'd just been sweeping, and there was a rat with its nose in a bag of mouldy tomatoes. I tiptoed into the stockroom and told Wally, intending only that he might witness the creature should Mr Brackley question my eyesight. Wally, however, immediately rushed into the shop and told Mr Brackley – Mr Brackley and several nearby customers. Several nearby customers abandoned their baskets and hurriedly left the shop. The shop manager pushed the lad through the door which led to the stockroom, through the stockroom, through the door which led from the stockroom and out onto the loading bay. Here, I believe, the lad was to have been unloaded, told to take his track bike and go. Luckily for Wally, at that moment the Man from Head Office emerged from the staff room with a mug of coffee and a request to speak to Mr Brackley.

'I'll be with you immediately, sir,' he grovelled. 'Don't say anything about rats,' he whispered to the lad and me before disappearing into the stockroom.

'Where's this bloody rat, then?' Wally bellowed.

'Back in that nest,' I supposed, pointing at the enormous pile of rubbish which still accumulated on the border between us and Burtons.

'Well, I'll wait for the bastard,' he declared.

'What for, Wally?'

From behind a stack of cardboard Wally retrieved the

short iron bar with which he'd so callously committed ratricide. 'Guess,' was all he said as he laughed the same manic laughter I'd last heard on the night of the flying liver sausage.

By now the water in my bucket was becoming too cool for car-washing and, anyway, rat-catching was a much more exciting prospect. Wally and I leaned against the Zephyr's bonnet and waited. We were very still and very silent. But not for long. Soon a rat tentatively poked its head out of a hole, sniffed the air, failed to detect our presence or Wally's feet and followed its nose towards the bag of mouldy tomatoes. Wally's blood lust immediately changed him from The Eastcote Greaser to Ratman, The Crepe Crusader, as he let out a demonic cry and hurled the iron bar at the unsuspecting rat.

During my lifetime there have been quite a few occasions when I know I might have died, but I never came nearer to an early departure from this world than that Thursday afternoon in Ruislip. Wally's missile missed the rat, struck a fence post and rebounded toward me at the speed of life. As it flashed past, only centimetres away from killing me, reality was replaced by some scratched frames from a surreal film. For what could only have been approximately 2.36 seconds I was an ice-cold, frightened spectator. Did I have an out-of-body experience? God only knows. I only know I had a near-miss experience, which is more than can be said for the Ford Zephyr. After the iron bar caressed my right ear it crashed right through the windscreen I was meant to have cleaned, showering glass all over shining bonnet, deranged Ratman and transfixed me.

Within seconds Mr Brackley burst upon this ugly incident, closely followed by the Man from Head Office. Both stared at the shattered windscreen as they rushed onto the loading bay, which was understandable but not very sensible. Our Man from Head Office kicked over my bucket of cold soapy water and sprawled headfirst off the loading bay. Fortunately for him, he flew through the air and belly-flopped onto a sea of cardboard. Unfortunately for Mr Brackley, most of the contents of the bucket flew in his direction, soaking his trousers, socks and shoes. While the Man from Head Office struggled against a cardboard tide, Mr Brackley trod water. They looked apologetically at each other. They stared conspiratorially at us. They were not happy men. Ten minutes later Wally and I doubled the number of unhappy Home & Colonial employees. We got the sack.

The rats were happy, though. When the loading bay was free of Man and manager, Saturday boy and Crepe Crusader, they laughed like shop assistants, splashed each other in a shallow pool and stuffed tomatoes.

I think Wally joined the Army next, probably a demolition regiment. I don't know what became of the rats, but a little later the manager and his wife also left the Home & Colonial. One afternoon Mr Brackley phoned my dad to say he was managing a supermarket in Sudbury and ask if I'd like a weekend job, working a couple of hours after school each Friday and all day Saturday. I was not consulted about this but Dad immediately accepted on my behalf. In return he probably offered Mr Brackley 'a pair of comps for the new show', two free tickets for the latest in a long line of Piccadilly Theatre flops. No doubt they conducted this conversation with telephones held in a special grip and feet placed at the right angle, arranging to seal the deal with a drink in an anonymous suburban saloon bar after a midweek Lodge meeting.

In the early sixties there were few large supermarkets in high streets, even fewer shopping precincts and no hypermarkets. Sainsbury in Ruislip was still an old-fashioned shop, one in which the customers had to queue at several counters – cheese, bacon, cake and biscuits, for example – where shop assistants served them. Most shops were like this, and any supermarkets were tiny compared to even

117

a modest 1990 establishment. The Home & Colonial was the largest supermarket in the Ruislip area, and considered to be superior to cut-price places like Victor Value and Tesco. Most of these 'inferior' shops sought to attract customers by offering low prices and trading stamps. The small C & Q supermarket in Sudbury which Mr Brackley now managed was definitely in the same division as these.

C & Q stood for Cut and Quality, but those initials mean Cycling and Queer for me. Let's get Queer out of the story before imagination leads to speculation and possible disappointment. I used to spend a lot of my time and money in a nearby second-hand bookshop which was run by two queers. ('Gay men' hadn't emerged from the dictionary at that time.) One of them took a fancy to me, and always stopped whatever he was doing to speak to me whenever I walked in. I took advantage of this situation to purchase some old books at reduced prices, but I was wise enough to browse and bargain only when other people were around. I still have all the volumes bought from that bookseller, the original asking price pencilled on an inside page. A couple are over two hundred years old, but I don't know if they are valuable or not.

Cycling next. I used to race to Sudbury on my Claud Butler, often timing myself in a vain attempt to emulate Tommy Simpson. I always struggled to beat the stopwatch on my way there, even with a tail wind, and I arrived late more often than a 97 bus. Just like the ill-fated Tommy Simpson, it was a long climb which ultimately defeated me.

There are two Sudburys in Middlesex, Sudbury Town and Sudbury Hill. My only route to C & Q in Sudbury Town was up through Sudbury Hill, and getting to the summit always had me struggling for breath and excuses. I usually stopped half a mile from the supermarket to wipe my hands on my bicycle chain so I could tell Mr Brackley, 'Sorry I'm late. Chain again. I must tighten it properly next time.' My black and oily hands served another useful purpose, the minutes I took to scrub them clean being minutes away from working in the shop.

I still had to keep the back yard tidy, but in Sudbury Town I also 'served'. Mr Brackley obviously felt I'd spent a long enough apprenticeship breaking up boxes and stacking shelves, so one Friday he instructed me in the arts of weighing, wrapping, display and customer relations, and five minutes later he let me loose on the shoppers of Sudbury. I used to work on a bacon/vegetable counter, weighing and wrapping greenback and streaky in between handling Jersey potatoes and carrots. I'm amazed at what those shoppers put up with, and occasionally wonder about how much food poisoning I caused. If the shop was busy I never had time to go to the staff room and wash my dirty hands but I always remembered the importance of good customer relations and apologized. The shoppers of Sudbury, though, preferred quick service to clean fingernails and I remember only one man insisting I wash and scrub my hands before weighing him three-quarters of smoked shortback.

I was weighing bacon on a Friday evening when a customer gave me the news of the shooting of John F. Kennedy in Dallas. By the time I'd cycled home his death had been announced. Mum told me as I opened the back door. It was painted yellow in 1962.

I didn't stay long at C & Q, the cycling and Mr Brackley getting right up my teenage nose. By 1963 I'd begun to work fairly regularly at the Piccadilly Theatre, anyway, so I wasn't in such great need of funds. I'd also started going to pubs and parties at weekends, and didn't want to have to race home from Sudbury, hurry through a meal, get myself ready and then rush out. Furthermore, if I had too much to drink on a Friday I wouldn't feel much like serving sprouts and streaky bacon the following morning. I started phoning Mr Brackley quite regularly on Saturdays, inventing an illness here and a family outing there, until the inevitable occurred. He sacked me. Again. I wasn't unhappy but Dad was. The way that he went on about the shame of me being dismissed by a fellow funny handshaker made me out to be as wretched as a certain war minister. I wonder if my sacking was sealed with a drink in an anonymous suburban saloon bar after a midweek Lodge meeting.

Up until the time I began teaching in Bristol in 1973 I had various holiday and weekend jobs. The most boring was loading lorries in the despatch department at Hales Cakes in Clevedon, and the most enjoyable was running a playgroup with Ros at Harefield Hospital. The hardest and dirtiest work I did was as a scaffolder's labourer on a building site next to Ruislip Gardens station, but that job was also the best-paid. The worst-paid was probably relief caretaker at a school in Ruislip, but I did get time to put my feet up and read a few books. Each job, even the most mundane, brought me into contact with people who could fuel my imagination. If I'm given the strength and time I'll write about working a ward away from Magdi Yacoub, world-famous heart transplant surgeon, or life with Jack Jessop, the infamous Geordie scaffolder of Earls Court. Dare you suppose that either could fuel my imagination like Miss Astell or Wally Medhurst?

January 19 1984

Eleanor Simone, hey baby,
what you doing now?
The wind is howling out at sea
and we're just waiting for you.

Eleanor Simone, honey,
how can you dance so late at night,
rolling like a ship in a storm?
Will you tango when you are born?

Eleanor Simone, baby,
are you listening now?
Can you hear us playing names
while we're just waiting for you?

Eleanor Simone, hey Eleanor,
light and words,
music, the sun and stars
are all just waiting for you.

Eleanor Simone, you kicker,
don't you give us extra time.
Once we've heard that whistle
we'll just want to take you home.

Eleanor Simone, hey baby,
what you doing now?
The wind is howling out at sea
And we're just waiting for you.

MUSICAL STARTING POINTS

At six o'clock on the day you were born, Eleanor, I was at a football meeting in a Bristol pub, having reluctantly left you with an exhausted mum in Bristol Maternity Hospital. I celebrated your arrival with a couple of pints of bitter and a bag of crisps, before returning to hospital where I found mother and child being photographed by proud new grandparents. Ros still looked tired but you were wide awake and staring at your world. Even then you went to bed late!

I used to visit twice a day, just to make sure that your mum was looking after you properly. On 7 February, after seeing you in the afternoon I drove to Bath and treated myself to a meal in a restaurant. Then I went shopping and bought three records, one for each of us. Mine was a jazz album featuring Red Rodney and Ira Sullivan, and I got the most recent Carly Simon release for Ros. When we took you home to Clevedon a couple of days later, I was so happy that I put the Carly Simon LP on our stereo and danced around the lounge with you.

'Touch' by Eurythmics was the third record, and was intended to be the very first in your own collection. I thought it would be a nice idea to buy for you whatever was the number one album each 6 February, and in 1984 it was 'Touch'. I subsequently bought you 'Agent Provocateur' by Foreigner (1985), 'Brothers in Arms' by Dire Straits (1986) and Paul Simon's 'Graceland' (1987). When I was no longer able to visit record shops Ken took over buying the rest of your collection: Terence Trent Darby (1988), New Order (1989) and Phil Collins (1990). I hope you'll enjoy collecting records in this way, but don't cheat by buying anything other than the number one album on your birthday!

My own record collection has always been fairly catholic in content, but with a distinct over-representation of Nina Simone and avant-garde jazz. In the last five or six years I have expanded my classical collection beyond a token Stravinsky and the odd Berlioz. Like most of my generation, the pleasure of the classical repertoire came to me after years of a different musical diet.

My record collection is also a catalogue of memories, since I can remember when and where I bought most of them. My first ever purchase was gospel music, 'Come in the room' by Clara Ward, bought in a sale in a Newcastle-upon-Tyne department store in the summer of 1963, at least two years before I owned a record player. My first Nina Simone LP, 'Forbidden Fruit', was bought in Claude Gill in Oxford Street, next door to the shop in which I worked, the Shoe Rack. At the same shop I also bought a 'Leadbelly Box', and 'The In Crowd' by the Ramsey Lewis Trio. When the record department manager in Claude Gill stopped giving me a discount I collected and bargained elsewhere.

A favourite place was a second-hand lock-up stall in Newport Court near Leicester Square station, between Gerrard Street and Charing Cross Road. It was right next to Waller's Clothes, where my dad bought most of his suits and I once purchased a pair of camel-coloured, straight-legged, pleat-fronted Daks trousers with turn-ups. This was at a time when all my contemporaries were in billowing flares, loons or hipsters! My musical choice was even less like my friends' than my trousers. At a time when they were buying Simon and Garfunkel, Bob Dylan, the Byrds or the Small Faces, I was listening to John Coltrane, MJQ, Thelonius Monk and Gary Burton.

There were no facilities for hearing records in Newport Court so I had to read sleeve notes carefully to determine whether I might like the music they described. I rather enjoyed this bran-tub method of buying LPs, choosing a record because it had an interesting line-up of both musicians and instruments or, much more likely, because it had an original cover design. It was here that I bought Wes Montgomery for the first time, 'Road Song', and Quincy Jones's 'Walking in Space'. One wet Saturday afternoon between shows at the Piccadilly I bought a Gabor Szabo album because it included several versions of Lennon and McCartney songs. Hunter Clarke, a diminutive stagehand at the theatre, thought I was wasting my money buying records in such a speculative fashion.

Hunter spent his money in West End pubs rather than record shops. In 1972, after we'd not seen each other for about three years, we went for a beer in the Round Table, near the New Theatre stage door. We were promptly refused service and summarily ordered out, Hunter having tried to fight with the landlord after he'd had too much to drink a few weeks earlier. The thought of Hunter, who made Brenda Lee look gigantic, sizing up to the tall Scots publican made me laugh, but the thought of that Scots publican depriving me of a pint of Tartan wasn't quite so funny.

'I'm Harry Pegg's son,' I protested. 'I'm always drinking in here with the lads from Wyndhams.'

'I don't care if you're Harry Lauder's maiden aunt, and you drink with the Boys in the Band, laddy,' was the response.

Protest as I did, I wasn't allowed to remain in that pub. Hunter and I were forced to drink and talk over old times in the nearby Salisbury, amidst splendid Edwardian mirrors and more band boys than I'd ever seen gathered together in one place.

I think that Hunter was also with me when I bought Stan Tracey's 'Under Milk Wood Jazz Suite', now a rare and valuable collectors' piece. Despite Hunter's criticism I never regretted buying any records from Newport Court although one or two, like John Tchicai's 'Cadentia Nova Danica' with its uterine cover illustration, are only played once a decade. A favourite purchase, 'The Amazing Amanda Ambrose', disappeared from my bedroom at the same time as my first Nina Simone album. Both were stolen by my kleptomaniac brother, Mike, to be swapped, no doubt, for twenty Embassy and a copy of *Parade*.

Unlike many of my friends, I never bought singles. This was because we didn't have a record player at home until 1965 when my dad bought one from a second-hand electrical goods shop in the Edgware Road. It was an American model, with two detachable speakers which delivered a passably good stereophonic sound. Unfortunately, if often went wrong and therefore spent almost as much time in an Edgware Road workshop as it did at home. I can't remember if the record player was bought just for me or for the three eldest children to share, but I had almost exclusive use of it, much to Mike's annoyance. I suppose that it wasn't surprising, therefore, that he sought to avenge himself by decreasing the size of my record collection.

The singles that stir my memory, then, are the ones that I heard on the radio at different times and places. The earliest were heard on *Children's Favourites*, on Saturday mornings as I ate my breakfast and dubbined my football boots before the weekly match. This was always played between Ruislip Rovers and Grant United down at the rec. by Ruislip Gardens railway station, and always ended with Rovers winning by a huge margin, something like 16–6. Despite this, Barry Grant's team turned up every Saturday morning, determined to register their first win. We Rovers had nearly all the best players, though, and were captained by Victor 'George' Holden. George was a Blackpool supporter, could dribble like Stanley Matthews and score goals like Stan Mortensen. He was also the only boy with a real leather football. Whenever I hear the much-requested Children's Favourite, 'The Runaway Train', I'm reminded of those 1958 days when steam trains were still so commonplace that they never distracted two teams of boys chasing George's leather football through wet grass on a Saturday morning.

In 1958 there was still a main-line platform at Ruislip Gardens, although trains rarely stopped there. The wooden platform was a favourite spot for messing about with my friends. We used to crawl underneath it, put pennies on the railway track and wait for a train to squash them. We also placed stones on the track – just small ones – and watched them being crushed. It was never our intention to derail a train but we were, on reflection, pretty stupid. Not only did we endanger the lives of people on the train, but if an 'accident' had occurred we would surely have been squashed as flat as our pennies.

Other Children's Favourites, like 'Hello, My Darling', 'Billy Goats Gruff' and 'The Laughing Policeman' recall what we had for breakfast as much as the football matches that followed. There was always porridge in winter and cornflakes in summer; occasional eggs, mainly poached and rarely scrambled; egg fried bread, fried bread and beans, beans on toast, toast and marmalade, marmalade on fried bread. And in an age of Silver Shred, Golden or Lemon Shred, sweet Shreds in jars that made me wince, Mum gave us thick and chunky tinned Seville marmalade.

Whenever I hear the singles of my teenage years I'm reminded of people and places, too, not just food or football. Hearing the Beatles' 'Love Me Do' makes me think of milk bottles at my secondary school, Vyners in Ickenham. While gulping milk straight from the bottle one morning break, the Fab Four first became a talking-point, replacing Steptoe impressions and speculation about Diane Rogers's bra size.

'You dirty old man.
Yeah, yeah, yeah.
With a bust like that,
you know it can't be bad.'

'Eleanor Rigby' recalls the hot summer of 1966. 'All the
lonely people, where do they all belong?' seemed to be the
plea from every Carnaby Street boutique when I worked
in a shoe shop there. Each establishment contributed its
own sounds to The Street – the Beach Boys, the Hollies,
Aretha Franklin, Fontella Bass, Cat Stevens or Manfred
Mann, in addition to the near-compulsory Beatles. Just to
be different, as usual, however, I entertained our customers with Herbie Mann, John Coltrane and Milt Jackson.
The other staff preferred soul or blues or ska or rock –
probably even Ken Dodd – to jazz, but I supplied the
record player so I chose what went on the turntable.

Incidentally, the record player was not the American
one my dad had bought. That was sitting in a workshop in
the Edgware Road. The record player I took to Carnaby
Street came from my school. Each Friday I would ask my
English teacher, David Rees, if I could borrow an Argos
recording of a Shakespeare play, together with a school
record player. David never questioned my interest in the
Bard, just wondered why my essays failed to improve.
The fact that I never once listened to a complete recording was why. 'Eleanor Rigby' always recalls that deception
that summer, when I was more interested in selling shoes
than writing essays, when I preferred the study of mini-
skirts and leggy girls to *Othello* or *King Lear*.

A strangely-titled song, 'Um, Um, Um, Um, Um,
Um, Um, Um' by Wayne Fontana and the Mindbenders,
reminds me of another two teachers at Vyners. Mr
Harries taught History and, being Welsh, helped with
rugby during Games lessons. He was enthusiastic about
both sport and subject but, like many Welsh teachers I've
met, his accent was broad and his voice soporific. He

also had an infuriating habit of interspersing everything he said with 'Um', and not just the eight 'Ums' of the song title. That would have been acceptable. No, sometimes it seemed as if there were as many 'Ums' in a Harries history lesson as political prisoners in Stalin's Russia. Some pupils only kept awake during his monologues by counting 'Ums'.

One Monday morning Mr Harries's boring reputation was shattered by the news that he'd married my tutor, Miss Naylor, at the weekend. I wonder how many 'Ums' found their way into 'Will you marry me, Eileen Naylor?' Nobody in the tutor group had known anything about their wedding plans so we'd not bought a present. I'm sure that someone soon organized a collection and bought a gift, though, because Miss Naylor was a very popular tutor.

Funnily enough, I almost ruined the secrecy of her big day when, in our tutor room on the Friday before the wedding I asked her, 'Are you doing anything tomorrow afternoon?' Miss Naylor's face immediately reddened and she hoarsely whispered, 'Why? What do you mean?' What I meant was I had two dress-circle comps for the Saturday matinée at the Piccadilly. Her reaction, though, made me think that she thought I was asking her out and my face also reddened. I stuttered and stumbled through an explanation, Miss Naylor relaxed, smiled and declined my offer. Her secret stayed a secret and I gave the comps to David Rees.

Thank your lucky stars that Scott Mackenzie is rarely on the radio singing, 'If you're going to San Francisco, be sure to wear some flowers in your hair.' Yuk! Whenever I have the misfortune to hear those words I am reminded of the kaftans, headbands and jingling bells that comprised the uniform of any self-respecting sixties hippy. Gathered together in Trafalgar Square or around Eros in Piccadilly Circus, the flower children were very much a tourist attraction, rivals to 'The Happy Wanderers' bandsmen and the Hare Krishna chorale. Some harmless hippies wore flowers behind their ears and drew peace symbols on their bodies; women flopped unsupported beneath their tie-dye Madras cotton tops; men grew droopy Zapata moustaches; some wore grimy 'South Sea Bubble' loons. The air in London seemed to be forever heavy with the scent of patchouli oil, the smell of Gitanes and marijuana, the stink of feet and foreign armpits. I tried to avoid rush hour in the Underground.

I enjoyed the grubby exotica that the hippies contributed to West End summers, but was less tolerant of their suburban clones. Kaftans seemed somewhat incongruous in Uxbridge, face paints were out of place in Ickenham and love beads definitely ill-met by Northolt. I clearly recall one example of my intolerance when I was queuing for a bus at Ruislip Station. A hippy ran past to catch a train, his hair floating behind his floral collar, the bells around his neck warning the ticket collector of his imminent arrival. After the bells had passed me I shouted, 'Unclean, unclean,' and looked for approval in the eyes of the ladies waiting with me for a 97 bus. Alas for the intolerant teenage cynic standing amongst them, their thoughts were on the price of cauliflowers and what to cook for tea. Bus queues are stony ground for biblical references.

I was never an Elvis Presley fan but I can remember when he assailed my musical consciousness. Barry Clegg was one of my best friends, and lived further down Stafford Road at number 83. Like me he came from a large family – large, that is, by comparison with other Ruislip Gardens families in the 1950s. In 1956, when I was eight, the Cleggs comprised Mr Clegg, aged about thirty-five; Mrs Clegg was a few years younger but looked ten years older; two girls – Pat, about thirteen, and Iona, four; and the boys – Barry, ten, Rolston (known as Rowley), eight, and Nigel, five. Mr Clegg worked at London Airport, and lived most of his non-working hours down at the Bell in New Pond Parade. He was small, stooped, and never seen coughing up and down Stafford Road without a cigarette for company. Mr Clegg rarely spoke to his family and left all discipline to his Irish wife.

Mrs Clegg worked as a cleaner, in several places, I think. The tidying of her own home was left to Pat, an unenviable task in the face of the three unruly Clegg boys and their gang of friends that came to visit, make toast, read Mr Clegg's American magazines and listen to Pat's Elvis albums. Those early RCA LPs would fetch a King Creole's ransom nowadays. At least they would in any sort of half-decent state, but nothing remained half-decent for long in Barry's house. For example, I remember when he and I went up into the loft to explore by candlelight. I dropped the candle and in the draughty darkness Barry tripped and put a foot through the ceiling of his sisters' bedroom. Years later the temporary Sellotape repair was still there, brown and just beginning to curl away from the cracked plaster.

I also remember when the red and white Venetian blinds in the front room went up, one Wednesday after-noon in 1957. Then they went down. And up. Down and up, down and up as Rowley and Barry tested them to near-destruction. Before that year had ended the blinds were less than half-decent, permanently down, never dusted, discoloured by Mr Clegg's cigarettes and fumes from the much-abused paraffin heater that stood on the hearth. The Clegg boys and I abused the heater by lighting rolled-up pages of the *Daily Mirror* to carry to the kitchen, to ignite the gas on the grill, to char the toast upon which to heap baked beans, to carry back to the front room and spill on the sofa.

When the adults were absent we also abused the par-affin heater by creating draughts of air which caused it to shoot flames like a dragon. We did this by either rapidly opening and closing the door a number of times or 'wafting' with one of Mr Clegg's magazines in the manner of a Boy Scout kneeling before the embers of a camp fire. What a fire the Cleggs' house would have made, and all of us along with its contents: the bean-splattered sofa and matching vinyl chairs; all the toast crumbs in the front room rug; the lino in the kitchen; half-eaten Sunblest, Echo margarine, 99 tea; the dog asleep under the kitchen table; the uncarpeted wooden staircase; the unmade beds, the magazines underneath Mr Clegg's side, the Madonna that slept above Mrs Clegg's tired head; the pink nylon hairbrush used to untangle Iona's waist-length yellow hair; all Pat's Elvis records.

We would definitely have been headline-of-the-week in the *Ruislip–Northwood Post*, an ill-defined photograph of the remains of 83 Stafford Road beneath FOUR BOYS DIE IN FIRE. Instead we all grew up (but how much?) moved away (but how far?) and played with fire in other rooms.

I know nothing much about the subsequent history of Pat, Iona, Rowley or Nigel. Mrs Clegg carried on cleaning other people's houses while her sons tinkered with the engine of a Ford Consul on blocks outside the house. When they disappeared with their father down to the Bell, she sang to herself and gardened. If she was in her front garden when I walked by Mrs Clegg was always ready with a smile and a genuine enquiry after my progress at college. Sadly, she died soon after I started teaching in Bristol so I never again got to chat with her. I hope she has her feet up in heaven.

Barry left school at fifteen and worked at Wall's in East Acton. We still went to the cinema together from time to time but gradually grew apart. I think he got himself an old car, probably that Consul parked on blocks outside the house. Later he got a girlfriend, and a little later he got into trouble. The last time we spoke at length was on a Central Line train to 'town'. As we passed Wormwood Scrubs he scratched his head and sagely said that life in prison must be worse than sharing a bedroom with his two brothers. He implied that he had experienced a period of custody somewhere, but I was unable to question him about either crime or punishment as he got off the train at the next station.

'Work or girlfriend?' I enquired as he stood up. Barry just smiled. Probation officer, more likely.

Nearly all early Elvis records bring to mind the Clegg family but one particular song, 'Jailhouse Rock', switches on a different memory. This is the only pop song that I remember my dad singing, his only nod in the direction of something 'with-it'. These days much music appeals to a wide audience so that, for example, a mother and her daughter may go to the same Barry Manilow concert – no mother and daughter of my acquaintance, I hope – but the divide between adult tastes and teenage culture was more marked in 1956. My parents, and the parents of all my friends, were old, and most certainly not 'with-it', so my dad's performance was definitely memorable.

He was out in the hall, making a telephone call and smoking a cigarette. It was a Saturday morning and I had just walked down the stairs; Mum was cooking breakfast; the radio was on and an announcer read a request for 'Jailhouse Rock'; Dad put down the telephone and began to wail. You should have seen that old man rock.

There are two aspects of this scene which are worth elaboration. Firstly, Dad was smoking, a habit he gave up within a year when he grew guilty about sending us children out to buy cigarettes for him. A pity my mum was never stricken by the same pangs of conscience. Instead, ignoring all medical evidence and the pleas of her eldest son, she continued to abuse her own body and pollute the air we all had to breathe. At the time of 'Jailhouse Rock' Dad smoked between thirty and forty cigarettes a day but when he decided to stop he literally gave up overnight.

Thereafter he allowed himself the occasional large cigar, sometimes after a meal and always at Christmas. These large cigars were given to him in boxes of twenty or more by business associates, and were kept in the top of Dad's wardrobe. When Mike discovered this hiding place he began to remove the odd King Willem for himself and his cronies to share round a campfire in the fields and woods nearby. Since Dad might go as much as twelve months without a cigar it took him a long time to realize the extent to which his stock had become depleted. However, he didn't need long to track down the culprit and my brother was duly punished. Unfortunately, he never learned from his mistakes and subsequently moved from one petty crime to another, regularly being caught but somehow avoiding getting into serious trouble.

The second detail of that Saturday morning scene worth elaboration is the telephone. I expect that most Ruislip Gardens homes have their own telephone today, but in 1956 we were one of the few families to have one installed. Those without their own telephone used a public call box. I think that there were five to serve the whole of Ruislip Gardens, the nearest to us being close by the Juniors' entrance gates at the school in Stafford Road.

Once our neighbours knew we had a telephone we became a message delivery service:

'Hello, Mrs Pegg, it's Mr Lucas here. Sorry to trouble you but would Steve be kind enough to pop down and tell Mrs Lucas I'll be late tonight. I've got to run a relief bus over to Hanwell. Thanks a lot.'

And then there were the knocks on the front door and a request to use the phone from someone like Mrs Costard:

'Sorry to bother you, Mrs Pegg, but our Ian's put his head through a window. Maureen's with him. Can I ring for an ambulance, please?'

Of course, we helped whenever we could and very few people ever tried to take advantage of us. Pat and Diane Taylor gave our telephone number to some boyfriends but Mrs Taylor soon discouraged their abuse of our messenger service; Mrs Costard seemed to be forever requesting ambulances, but no-one ever minded assisting her as she single-handedly brought up her family following her husband's sudden death; Mrs McDonald came nearest to being a nuisance, but the eccentric Irishwoman amused us so much that we never banned her.

Eventually, most of our neighbours became telephone subscribers, thereby depriving us of first-hand knowledge of accidents and scandal, bereavements and birthdays, holiday plans and health problems which we'd overheard from just behind the front room door. The television would be turned down imperceptibly as our ears strained to detect every last intimate detail. Until it became too intimate, and then Mum would turn up the volume and ask, 'Who wants a cup of tea? Julie, put the kettle on, please.'

After his rendition of 'Jailhouse Rock' my dad's voice was heard less frequently, rock and roll replaced by songs from the shows – *Oliver, Blitz, Enrico, Fiorello, Strike a Light, I and Albert, The Young Visiters, Man of Magic, Man of La Mancha*. If a show was successful and enjoyed a long run my dad might learn some of the words of one or two songs, but since the names of his own children eluded him with alarming ease the chances of him singing along with Keith Michell or Richard Kiley amounted to something of an impossible dream.

He soon learned tunes, however, so whistled cheerily around the best West End streets – like Brewer, Berwick, Old Compton, Denman, L'Isle and Rupert – on his way to a theatre or pub. Grown showmen and ambitious stagehands learned to recognize his whistling style so that they could down a swift pint and evacuate a crowded bar before Harry Pegg found them and announced,

'They've called Beginners. Get your skates on.' Anyone who missed a cue was usually sacked on the spot, so I always made sure that I was on stage for mine. Mike was not so good at time-keeping, though, and was once sacked for being in the Queen's Head with a pint of lager and another showman when he should have been helping with a scene change. No family favouritism there!

Despite his love for whistling a catchy tune, Dad never whistled on stage as this was considered to be unlucky. According to him this superstition originates from the time when cues from the stage manager were whistled through lengths of tube which connected the prompt corner to showmen on the stage and in the flies. Any extraneous whistling would lead to confusion and was, therefore, prohibited.

When I was at my primary school pop music was just something in the background, always there but less important than what was for tea or the kick-off time of the next football match. I was once in a skiffle group, though, hastily formed for a class party when I was eleven. I played a swanee whistle and loaned Mike Bozier our ukelele; David Barker improvised a drum set from pots and pans; Paul Butler strummed a pretty mean pink plastic guitar. Someone else borrowed his mum's washboard, a couple of boys joined in with comb-and-toilet-paper kazoos, and we played along with a 78 record of 'Red Sails In The Sunset'. We weren't called back for an encore.

It was only after I went to grammar school that music became something worthy of inclusion in everyday conversations. We compared the Shadows with the Ventures, Eden Kane with Bobby Darin; we Brylcreemed and combed our hair as near to the style of our current hero as the unfashionable teaching staff permitted; some of us stood in front of the mirror in the boys' toilets and snarled, sang, twisted, trembled, pouted and posed our

135

way through versions of the top ten smash hits of the time, gems like:

'The weather man says "Clear today", he doesn't know you've gone away and it's raining, raining in my heart.'

'Well, I ask you, what a way to treat a guy, what a way to cheat and lie because I wanted you.'

'Hey there darling, how about a date? Let's go round a coffee bar, I know one that ain't too far.'

'So I went to the chaplain, and he authorized me to send for my Ebony Eyes.'

'I don't wanna four-leaf clover, I don't wanna old horse shoe. I want your kiss coz I just can't miss with a good luck charm like you.'

Our imitations of Eddie Cochrane, Elvis, Cliff Richard or Buddy Holly were not performed to impress the girls who, although they had begun to occupy our imaginations, spent little time in our company. They seemed to divide their time between hairdressing, applying make-up and the comparison of petticoats. If they weren't backcombing huge bouffant homages to Dusty Springfield they were spitting in someone else's mascara; and if they weren't comparing steel combs in the girls' toilets they were grouped outside the senior mistress's room awaiting the compulsory daily petticoat inspection.

At this time of the twist, trad jazz, Aldermaston marches and Alma Cogan, it was fashionable for young ladies to wear several boned or sugar-starched petticoats beneath their skirts. Unfortunately for Vyners girls, the maximum permitted number of plain unstiffened petticoats was one, and any excess garments caught in the act of being fashionable were confiscated by Miss Holmes, the senior mistress. She was a stern and humourless career rule-maker, fonder of petty regulations than petticoats. I never thought much about her character in 1961, but now I wonder if there wasn't some unhappiness in her earlier life which made her such a miserable and unsmiling person. Perhaps, like the enigmatic crippled ballet school principal in Julie's *Bunty*, her personality had been altered by an unexplained cruel twist of fate and she wasn't really as dry and uncaring as she appeared. Perhaps, too, she'd become so used to acting the role of stern spinster teacher that she lived the part each moment of her working day. If there was another side to Miss Holmes we never got to see it at school. She would always be an old and bitter Bette Davis, even if the young Ginger Rogers danced inside her heart.

I did once manage to make Miss Holmes smile with my schoolboy wit, when ten or twelve girls were outside her room as Brian Bardrick and I were on our way from tutor room to bike sheds at the end of the day. Guessing that the purpose of the gathering was the usual undergarment spot check, I shouted out in my best Max Miller voice, ''Allo! 'Allo! Now there's a funny fing. What's all this then, Petticoat Lane?' I waited just long enough for simultaneous group giggle and a rarely-observed smile before speeding away.

One morning Miss Holmes made the whole school smile. We were in the assembly hall awaiting the arrival of Mr Jagger, the headmaster, and his two deputies, Miss Holmes and Mr Fox. Between 1960 and 1967 I endured hundreds of uneventful Vyners assemblies – sat, stood, stared, sang, mimed, moaned, mumbled, muttered, listened, learned, laughed, looked, drowsed, daydreamed, dissented, played, prayed and yawned – but I would gladly sit, stand, stare, sing and so on through them all again just for the chance to see another performance of 'Carry On Dotty Holmes'. That performance began like any other unexciting assembly when Mr Jagger and his two deputies came through the door at the side of the stage and appeared before us, black gowns flowing, grim frowns showing. After the first formalities, however, the script took an unexpected turn for the memorable.

As Miss Holmes sat down her thoughts must have been somewhere else – with Fred Astaire on a Hollywood set, perhaps – and she somehow missed her chair. Tumbling backwards with all the athletic grace of Norman Wisdom, her little legs flew up in the air and wide apart, revealing to the world a pair of pink bloomers. Mr Jagger immediately stood up and commanded 'Don't laugh!' and no-one did. Vyners Grammar in the sixties was more compliant than Grange Hill Comp in the eighties. As Miss Holmes smoothed down her tweed skirt with agitated fingers, her face flushed and image crushed, the hall was so quiet you could have heard a fly fart. If just one person had dared to laugh the whole place would have erupted, I'm certain, but somehow everyone restricted themselves to the tiniest of smiles and Jagger returned to his script.

'The following boys have been awarded their non-qualified badge: Ronald Stubbs, Terence Wise, Bernard Bosher, Vaughan Merlyn and Stephen Pegg.'

During assemblies, most pupils stood in rows on the woodblock floor, boys on the right and girls on the left; sixth formers sat on chairs on the balcony at the rear of the hall; black-gowned tutors sat on both sides of the hall where they could supervise their tutor groups; teachers without tutor groups sat on the side balcony to the left of the main body of the hall; the Catholics, Jews, and any others who did not have to attend the corporate act of worship which followed the reading of notices, stood on this balcony, near to an exit door so that they might escape quickly when the headmaster gave the word.

While we waited Mr Lane, Head of Music, played some lively Liszt or cheery Chopin on the piano. Bearing in mind the tone of most of our school assemblies, I feel that the Berlioz 'March to the Scaffold' might have been more appropriate. As Mr Lane's fingers flew across his keyboard he grinned with all the delight of a man who had forgotten that he was timetabled to teach 3F2 next.

Mr Lane never was able to convince me or most of my peers that Beethoven was better than the Beatles or Rachmaninov could give more satisfaction than the

Rolling Stones, but he did make us laugh when he called the composer Rimsky-Korsakov 'Rip Your Corsets Off'. Apart from that corny joke, I remember him for his deceptive spin bowling and jolly 'Two Ronnies' personality, smiling rosy-cheeked Corbett face atop seaside-postcard, beer-bellied Barker frame.

I remember some of the other teachers who waited in the hall with us. What notes would I have made about them for an end-of-term report?

BAXTER, 'Squadron Leader' (Physics): Recently retired from the Royal Air Force and retrained; unflappable under fire from the enemy, his heart was never in telling us about coil magnets or accumulators and his head was always somewhere else, just cruising at 30,000 feet.

BROADBRIDGE, Dickie (English): First of many teachers who encouraged me to write poetry, although the only one who advised me not to wait for the Muse but to 'Go out and ravish her'. He once picked me up and used me as blackboard rubber in 2F1 lesson; later introduced me to Dylan Thomas and translated 'Llaregub' for me. One morning, as two heavily-powdered girls passed us in the corridor, he confided that he 'preferred the honest sweaty smell of boys to the sickly sweet perfume of females' – must have been reading D. H. Lawrence at the time.

BROOKS, Mandy (English): Tall and blonde lady who was a fantasy Desdemona to my Iago. She used to take her baby into school, leaving a pram there each evening; when someone broke into Vyners one night the pram was used to carry away school trophies, both pram and swag ending up in nearby Swakeleys Lake.

COOPER, Miss (Latin): Large and eccentric lady who never went anywhere without enormous handbag/small suitcase containing enough chocolate bars and other snacks to feed a Roman legion, she never had the pleasure of teaching me Latin since I barely progressed beyond remedial French.

EVANS, Rhys (English): Another bag-carrier, his being so overloaded with exercise books that he walked everywhere bent over like the bell-ringer of Notre Dame. His hacking smoker's cough was made worse by carrying that bag up and down stairs and along miles of corridor, and I'm sure he left Vyners for health reasons, seeking a less arduous job in a single-storey school.

FERGUSON, Peter (English): Chaucer expert and excellent jiver (despite turned-up toes), his reading of *Lord of the Flies* in 1963 included an excellent impression of a boy blowing into a conch shell. He was a very enthusiastic shot-putter who was almost solely responsible for the replacement of a muddy mound with an all-weather throwing and jumping area. A balding, short man with poor eyesight, he later married Miss Woodmansey from the Art Department.

HALFPENNY, Mr (Maths): A very tall man who wore the most unfashionable suits for two terms each year, and white linen jacket with grey flannel trousers every summer term, he was a great exponent of 'chalk and talk'. Chalk dust accumulated all over his clothes while he talked in Algebraic to the blackboard, just occasionally glancing over his shoulder to ensure that Brian Bardrick was not making obscene gestures in the direction of Liz Andrews and Beryl Kelly. He cycled to school on an old pushbike which was probably a survivor of his undergraduate days, along with his suits, Brian Bardrick and I usually racing past him and his cycle clips near West Ruislip station. He must have had a sense of humour lurking somewhere amongst his Napier's Bones because he named his daughter Penelope – Penny Ha'penny!

HAMILTON, Clive (PE and Maths): It always amused

me that a man whose working life was devoted to improving boys' ability to run, jump, kick, throw, swim, trampoline, vault, bat, bowl, catch, maul, ruck, tackle, pass, spring, stretch, exercise and endure, should smoke as heavily as he did. Equally amusing was his own honest admission that he was studying for 'O' level Maths at the same time as he was teaching us the subject. Oddly enough he made more sense with his simplistic approach than some of the 'real' mathematicians. He rarely picked me for the First XI soccer team, even though I once scored a hat-trick against Abbotsfield, probably because I shouted at my own team better than I played.

KING, John (Biology): A no-nonsense cuffing type (termed 'good disciplinarian' in job references, no doubt); claimed that Hank Marvin was a neighbour.

KORNFELD, Dr (Chemistry): Grey-haired and quiet lady with mid-European accent which made her pronunciation of words like 'retort' and 'combustion' sound menacing. Some of us used to deliberately drop test tubes in her lessons and see who could break the most in one 'accident', Roger Collard dropping a whole rack of twelve to set a record in 1964.

LANE, Miss (English): The woman who taught me the difference between imply and infer always wore a deer-stalker hat when driving her Triumph Herald convertible – top down regardless of season! Miss Lane produced all the best school plays with the energy of Joan Littlewood and the wit of Noel Coward, and helped found the Compass Theatre in Ickenham.

McNEIL, Mr (Chemistry): A man with dandruff which sat on his shoulders like snow on a window-sill and earned him the nickname 'Dan', he liked his subject but his enthusiasm never rubbed off on me, only his dandruff as he leaned across the workbench to observe me dissolving copper sulphate crystals.

NAYLOR, Eileen (History): My tutor, she persuaded all the children in her tutor group to donate a small sum weekly to Save the Children Fund. I was nearly always in arrears but cleverly orchestrated peer-group pressure encouraged me to pay up. Miss Naylor loved discussions of a topical nature and once, during a debate on housing needs, she passionately argued the case for system-built tower blocks while I, in my usual flippant manner, pointed out the shortcomings of fire service turntable ladders in the event of fire. During most lessons she sat on top of the front desk, facing her class with legs crossed and feet placed on a chair, her long fingers clasped around her bony white knees. From time to time she would proclaim, 'Now people,' simultaneously uncrossing and recrossing her shapely legs to reveal a glimpse of white knicker to the cognoscenti who sat in the desks immediately in front of her.

REES, David (English): A Benjamin Britten fan, he taught me in the Sixth Form and was rightly critical of most of my 'A' level essays, often describing them as 'undisciplined'. When he first went to Vyners he drove a scruffy old Mini, later replaced by a brand new Mini, neither of which he ever washed. One year he chose me to make a speech at Prize Day, but had to rewrite my over-political vote of thanks to the chief guest and prize-giver, telling me that my version was 'undisciplined'.

ROBERTSON, Murie (Geography and Maths): Tall and handsome Scotsman, much fancied by many young ladies and much feared by most young men, who always insisted on a hand inspection before commencing any lesson, to prevent us smudging our books. Some pupils – but not me – joked that he mapped the contours of his shapely wife while she sang 'Nymphs and shepherds come away . . . for this is Flora's holiday.'

ROBERTSON, Pamela (Music): A dark-haired lady with the voice and the bust of an opera diva who wouldn't let us sing Lennon and McCartney songs instead of 'Nymphs and Shepherds'.

SPENCER, John (Art): Fond of cuffing boys heavily across the head, he was never seen without a shirt tail flapping out of the back of paint-spattered corduroy trousers; once queued for lunch with fly zip down; exhibited in London galleries; he liked to play records or listen to the radio in the art studio while we attempted to paint a still life of three apples, an orange, two bananas and a Mateus Rosé bottle; sometimes he took us outside school to make sketches, awarding our efforts with 'Six, Three or Nought'; his son John – a long thin print off the old woodblock – later attended Vyners; when questioned by me, Mr Spencer denied that Sir Stanley was a relative but said he knew of a good pub in Cookham.

TAYLOR, Angela (Girls' PE): An active and energetic all-round sportswoman who discouraged boys from playing tennis because of a shortage of courts; she also discouraged me from playing tennis with any girls because of my shortage of patience. I was so bad-tempered that between 1963 and 1966 I had more mixed doubles partners than John McEnroe has had fines. (Can I be serious?) In 1966 I began playing with Ros. She improved my temper – not by much, but enough for us to remain partners.

The governing triumvirate of Jagger, Fox and Holmes hadn't yet made an appearance in the hall. What recollections of these three are filed away in the bottom drawer of my brain?

JAGGER, Trevor (Headmaster): A very innovative and energetic, high-profile career educationalist who was more successful with rules than relationships. He taught me Physics, and always marked books with a green fountain pen. He insisted on the highest standards of dress from pupils yet always turned up for Saturday morning sports matches in old wellies and a raincoat borrowed from Worzel Gummidge. Mr Jagger held his very own detention sessions after school on Fridays, during which detainees had to copy long and boring passages from various scientific journals while he sat and picked his nose. Only those who, like me, held season tickets for 'Headmaster's Detentions' could verify this most unheadmasterly behaviour. In January 1960 I was the first ever Vyners pupil to be ordered by Jagger to stand up for ridicule in front of the whole school. This was after I'd thrown an empty tin can in the playground and badly cut Ian Manson's mouth. Later, in about 1964, he caned me after I had made an over-sensitive and highly dramatic female art teacher cry in class. He also told the parents of some of my friends that I was an unhealthy influence, and when I left school he wrote that I was the most ambivalent pupil he had ever come across. I don't think he liked me much.

HOLMES, Miss (Senior Mistress): A very miserable but industrious, low-profile career administrator who taught German with Teutonic efficiency. She liked to dress in tweed skirts, unfashionably tailored with the hemline well below her knees. She always wore Hush Puppy shoes, presumably to enable her to creep silently along corridors and pounce upon unsuspecting schoolgirl miscreants.

FOX, Mr (Deputy Head): 'Foxy' was one of the few teachers to be given an affectionate nickname by the pupils. Despite his fierce voice and intimidating walrus-like appearance he was very popular. He was a firm but consistently fair disciplinarian. He sometimes drove to school in his ancient black Rolls-Royce, a description of which could have applied equally well to its owner. It had definitely seen better days, the bodywork needing repair and the upholstery being frayed and patched. However, the engine was sound and reliable, even if it was smoky and had lost the acceleration it once boasted. Mr Fox loved rugby, and once drove some boys to Bristol in his car for a match against his previous school, Bristol Grammar. He also loved cricket, and each summer term rigged up a television set in his study so that he might be able to watch Test matches as he marked books or interviewed the odd errant young man. He travailed mightily to teach me French *mais sans beaucoup de success*, and in one of his lessons caught me hiding behind the largest boy in the first year, Bernard Matthews, when he was looking for a volunteer to *répondez, s'il vous plaît*. He warned me against ever attempting the same trick *encore*, and told the whole class that he had been a *professeur* for so long that he knew *toutes les avoidance techniques in le livre*. Despite this claim we never failed to sidetrack him during his Divinity lessons, much preferring listening to his Greek and Latin semantics to discussing Beatitudes or Miracles.

While the whole school impatiently awaited the arrival of these three and listened to Norman Lane or the school string group featuring the violins of Christine Broadhurst and Paula Mason, Mr Jagger was probably discussing with his deputies matters relevant to discipline and the efficient organization of the school.

AGENDA

1. Rising hemlines and the best place for girls' knees.
2. School caps in bus queues in Uxbridge.

3. The length of Harry Smith's hair.

4. Smoking in the toilets between lessons – reprimanding the staff concerned.

5. The unsuitability of black bras worn with white blouses.

6. The length of Geoff Roper's hair.

7. Affirmation of the school credo that 'Each pupil shall write with fountain pen only', and confirmation that ballpoint pens be prohibited.

8. Tony Gibney's moustache and Ray Sheppherd's beard.

9. Any other business: noise in the dining hall, running in the corridors, water in the toilets, fog in the afternoon, ice in the playground, money in the School Fund.

After the Politburo had discussed their final hairstyle and hemline, agreed to confront the male student teacher currently compromising his career prospects with a mature young lady in the Fifth Form, and shelved the indelicate subject of incinerator fumes, they left the headmaster's study and walked the short distance to the hall, entering the stage area through a side door.

When we heard that door open, those who had been sitting stood up respectfully, those who were already standing stood respectfully still, and those who had been whispering became resentfully silent. The Big Three stood behind their chairs, which had also been waiting in a row, each of them dusted and tucked underneath the polished refectory table that dominated the stage. School assembly was at last about to begin.

My memory of Vyners assemblies is probably distorted by all those I subsequently attended and conducted while I was a teacher, but I know that they always included some of the following elements.

1. The headmaster wished the school good morning and invited everyone to sit down. The non-worshippers

146

remained standing ready for their customary quick escape.

2. Notices were read by a deputy, a teacher, a tutor or a pupil, depending upon who was taking the assembly. These often included brief accounts of yet another mauling by Bishopshalt of all our rugby teams, or a loudly-fanfared success story about girls in a netball rally in High Wycombe.

3. 'Headmaster's Notices' were read by the head-master, of course, and were usually cautionary tales aimed at making even the most innocent individual feel waves of collective guilt. Quite often, though, the monstrous came with the mundane or trauma followed trivia, so Jagger's warnings fired all our imaginations. They were intended to stop us veering from the straight and narrow Vyners' way, but who could fail to be intrigued by the story of the boy who fell while sliding down banisters and broke a leg? And what about the Cruella de Ville of the Girls' Toilets who burgled a London store and was expelled for backcombing her hair in a manner likely to cause a breach of the peace? Then there was the young man who predated Hilda Margaret's Enterprise Initiative by twenty-five years and set himself up as a dealer in purple hearts. He was duly expelled and his crimes catalogued in a Headmaster's Notice, thereby bringing to the attention of an innocent majority of the school population the existence, availability and false glamour of drugs. Where is he now, that red-haired mod with the entrepreneur's eye? I heard that he'd been sent to prison. If he's out I can imagine him working at the Department of Health, organizing the sort of hip-replacement franchises that no-one could refuse and negotiating contracts with drug companies.

4. The non-worshippers were released and went and did whatever they did – rehearsed their Bar Mitzvah

speech, read about St Bernadette, drew designs for prayer mats . . .

5.   To comply with the terms of the 1944 Education Act our corporate worship consisted of a hymn, a reading from the Bible and at least one prayer. Those tutors who sat on the boys' side of the hall had both their faith and their eardrums tested by our broken-voiced croaking, and the canniest tutors always ensured that the sweetest-sounding first-year boys were at the end of the row nearest them. I was one of the silent dissenting minority who mimed along with the hymn of the day, although I used to enjoy contributing my flat monotone to the rousing school hymn 'For All the Saints'. I wonder how many of my fellow poseur-agnostics are now churchwardens, Sunday School teachers, lay preachers or just evangelized hymn singers?

6.   Very occasionally our act of corporate worship was followed by an act of contrived hymn practice. These were arranged, I suspect, so that the majority of the teaching staff could attend a hastily-arranged meeting to discuss something like the implications of the aforementioned drug dealing, or strategies to counter the increased incidence of peroxided hair, or – most likely – to finalize arrangements for the forthcoming summer fête.

7.   Sometimes the girls were kept in the hall at the end of assembly for 'Girls' Notices'. I imagine that these were a mixture of feminine hygiene information, reminders about uniform regulations and further cautionary tales.

'Last month you were warned about accepting sweets from complete strangers, and then incinerating the sweet wrappers. Well, the same person who witnessed some Vyners girls taking sweets has been in contact with us once more. Apparently last night she observed a Vyners girl on the eastbound platform of Hillingdon station talking to a very strange man who picked his nose while wearing a dirty old raincoat and wellington boots. That girl was NOT wearing her beret! You have been warned so many times about not wearing your beret . . .'

Just a poem for Jack's Sixth Birthday

I know a young Aussie who swallowed a fly.
I don't know why he swallowed a fly,
Perhaps he'll cry.

I know a young Aussie whose name is Jack,
One day in the garden I slapped his back.
I slapped his back when he swallowed a fly.
I don't know why he swallowed a fly,
Perhaps he'll cry.

I know a young Aussie from Emu Plains,
When I slapped his back he got terrible pains,
Pains in his throat, even more in his head,
Down his right arm and up his left leg,
Pains in his knees, neck – teeth – tum,
Pains in his nose, elbows and b. . .*

I know a young Aussie who just loved to eat
Everything from A for Apple to Zeebra meat.
He ate before breakfast and after his tea,
He could eat while whistling or swimming in the sea.
He ate kangaroo kebabs, poached platypus toes,
He even ate nachos while his sister picked her n. . .**

I know a young Aussie who swallowed a fly.
When he swallowed that fly
I never saw him cry.
I know a young Aussie who swallowed a fly.
I can guess why he swallowed that fly,
At least I can try.

I know a young Aussie whose name was Jack Plimmer,
When he looked in a mirror he thought he was thinner.
Out in the garden he swallowed a fly.

*   b stands for big thumb
** n stands for knickers off the floor

I can guess why he swallowed that fly,
At least I can try.

He swallowed that fly to eat as a snack,
But then I slapped him on the back.
When I slapped his back Jack felt terrible pains
From the tips of his toes to the top of his brains.
The pain in his brain made young Jack shout,
His mouth opened wide and the fly flew out.
The fly flew off to inform his mum
Of what he'd seen in that Aussie tum –

Half a dozen carrots, a pound of greens,
Two rice puddings and a tin of baked beans,
A sliced white loaf, a pair of blue socks,
Digestive biscuits still in a box,
Some mustard, a marble, a million processed peas,
Custard, apple crumble, mouldy blue cheese,
A *Spiderman* comic and a slice of Vegemite toast,
All the first-class stamps from last week's post.

I know a young Aussie who swallowed a fly.
Now I know why he swallowed a fly.
Hunger, that's why.

Just a story for Eleanor's Class

I sit
all day
on my own
in my tiny room
at the very top of
my very tall house down
at the bottom of a very steep
hill in this very old town where
I live very happily with my cat Mouse,
mouse Frog, frog Cat and a very old goldfish.

I sit
all day
on my own.
Time passes.
When days are warm
and the sky is very blue,
someone opens wide the window
in my tiny room at the very top of
my very tall house down at the bottom
of a very steep hill in this very old town
where I live very happily with my fat cat Mouse,
brown mouse Frog, pond frog Cat and a very old
　　　goldfish.

We count clouds.
Mouse can purr to nine.
Frog waves a tail to twenty.
Cat can croak to a million and one.
The goldfish isn't very good with numbers
but does have twenty-something swimming badges.

Sometimes
it seems as if
all the world wants
to drift in and join us –
silent writer, ginger Mouse,
Frog with whiskers, hopping Cat,
and a goldfish who spends every day
blowing noughts and kisses at the sky.
We stop counting clouds and listen, wait for
the sounds of the world in the town below to float
up and in, and then begin to fill our dreaming heads.

One
first-class postwoman with squeaking brakes,
swings my gate and stamps her feet.

Two
milkmen float by, bottles chinkling,
singing that song from *Annie*.

A trio
of sparrows sit upon a window ledge
and gossip like shopgirls.

Four
ballet dancers prance past,
hand in hand in two twos.

Five
local teachers stand on a corner
and tick themselves off.

Two, four, six
laughing butchers' boys
meet outside the chip shop.

Seven
mums with pushchairs stop for a chat;
their babies wake and stir and start.

Two, four, six, eight
little schoolgirls skip
and giggle in the park.

Three, six, nine
merry plumbers' mates
trip by in tap shoes.

Two, four, six, eight, ten
Shun! Quick marching soldiers
go up and down the hill.

One seaside postcard, from a friend;
two extra pints, tomorrow, please;
three short stories;
four pirouettes in pink tights;
five wrong answers;
six pork sausages;
seven wet nappies;
eight jellies on a plate;
nine hot taps and tails;
ten pairs of polished boots on parade.

Now is the time for someone to come and close
the window in my tiny room at the very top
of my very tall house down at the bottom
of a very steep hill in this very old
town where I live very happily with
that fat cat *****, brown mouse
****, croaking frog *** and
one very old ********.
We count stars.

154

By:
Eleanor

Just a poem for St Andrew's School

Lightweight – large – skinny – small –
Heavyweight – huge – tiny – tall –
Children are all shapes and sizes,
Giving teachers some odd surprises.
But just as children come and grow,
So every teacher will always know
In every class, in every school,
You cannot fail to find a fool.
And every teacher who's ever taught
Could list at least one other sort:
Girls and boys who solve their sums
With computers, toes and thumbs;
Smilers, spellers, story-tellers;
Kickers, criers, never-triers;
Writers, waiters, do-it-laters;
Readers, runners, full-of-funners;
Meanies, moaners, sit-aloners;
Joiners, jumpers, playground thumpers;
Touchers, talkers, blackboard chalkers;
Whizzkids, winners, extra dinners;
Sneezers, teasers, tops-at-tests;
Know-its, poets, pains and pests.

Keeley Kylie Samantha Lorraine
Really was a terrible pain,
Forever telling such whopping lies
Which gave her schoolfriends popping eyes.
Her teachers tried their very best
To change the fibbing female pest,
But Keeley Kylie Samantha Lorraine
Stayed St Andrew's naughtiest pain.

Once, one Wednesday after school,
Keeley was swimming at the pool
When, tired of going up and down,
She dressed herself and walked to town.

Just by Safeway she stopped to phone
And then, pretending she was home,
9 – 9 – 9, she slowly dialled.
A voice replied. She slyly smiled.

'Hello. Help! I need the aid
Of all the Clevedon Fire Brigade.
I'm in my house, quite near to you,
And locked inside the upstairs loo.
Down in the kitchen there's a fire
Which is quickly creeping higher.
Please, please hurry! I'm getting hot!
I'm so afraid I'll burn my bot!'

Firemen rushed from wide and near,
From the Prom and from the Pier;
From Kenn men came and from the Pill,
From Channel Road and Chapel Hill;
Postman, plumber, painter, printer;
Insurance man and local sprinter;
Dustman, busman, batsman, bowler;
Music master, rock and roller.

To their station those firemen flew,
And then towards that little girl's loo
Because they thought her all alone
And locked inside a blazing home.
Leaning ladders against her wall,
They waited ready should she fall,
But fibbing female wasn't within –
She was watching with evil grin,
Watching as water from fire brigade hoses
Flooded rooms and flattened roses.
She laughed so loud, like a mad hyena,
Two boys shouted, 'Look! We've seen her.'

Everyone stopped and turned to glare
At Keeley Kylie smiling there,
So very soon Samantha's face

Showed Lorraine in deep disgrace.
That smile just vanished on the spot
While she went both white and hot.

'You naughty girl!' her father said.
'No more swimming and straight to bed!'
'You naughty girl!' her mother raged.
'Kids like you should be kept in a cage!'
'You naughty girl!' five firemen bleated.
'We've never been so badly treated.'
'You naughty girl!' everyone called.
Keeley Kylie just stood and bawled.

When everyone shouted, 'Samantha Lorraine!
You naughty girl! You're such a pain!'
She decided there and then
She'd never make up tales again;
She'd change herself from teacher's pest
And try to be St Andrew's best;
And never-never-never 9-9-9
To waste-waste-waste a fireman's time.

SITTING IN THE STALLS, WAITING IN THE WINGS

I was more fortunate than all of the children in my school, and probably luckier than all but a dozen and one children born in Britain in 1948, in that from the age of two I was in and out of theatres even more than my brother Mike would subsequently be in and out of trouble. Most of my friends might have been taken to see a pantomime once or twice before puberty, but I had several theatrical experiences under my belt long before I had graduated from infants' school.

My dad was master carpenter at the 'Q' Theatre, near Kew Bridge, and I remember being shown the workshops and the backstage area when I was barely out of reins. I remember, too, sitting in a tiny bar at 'Q' after a Christmas show. My memory is aided, I readily admit, by regular viewing down the years of a black-and-white photo of Julie and me shovelling jelly and ice cream into our mouths as if we had never seen the stuff before, my sister cross-eyed and chewing her spoon, me all knees and embarrassment. I don't remember the name of the show, but it might have been directed by one of the Peters, Brook or Hall, and it almost certainly starred a Lockwood, dark-haired Wicked Lady Margaret or darling daughter Julia. Ask my dad and he'll tell you that Sean Connery was an assistant stage manager, Dirk Bogarde had one entrance and two lines, and Anton Diffring was a villain with a secret Nazi past.

According to Dad, any actor worth an Equity card had started his career at 'Q', and for years we only endured repeats of old British movies on our television in the hope

159

that Dad might recognize 'an old "Q" actor' and we might enjoy one of his repertoire of critical comments about the actor's performance or personality. This repertoire was limited and predictable, it's true, but enlivened many an otherwise tedious afternoon's viewing. Firstly, there was 'What a complete and utter load of punk!' (sometimes shortened to 'What a load of punk!' or even 'What punk!') which was always delivered with a despairing gesture of right hand banged open-palmed onto his forehead, then swept back behind and over his right ear. Secondly, whenever Dad recognized an actor he would leap out of his chair and exclaim 'I've worked with him!' If the 'him' concerned summoned up fond memories, we would be regaled with a tale that we had already heard a dozen times, and for which I would have to supply the names that Dad had forgotten since first telling it. If the memories of the actor were not good, usually because he was 'piesomeownius' (which we understood to mean that he never bought a round of drinks in the 'Q' bar) or 'queer' (which we didn't understand until about 1963) Dad's right index finger would be stabbed venomously at the television screen and some disparaging comments muttered into a clenched fist.

If Mum was sitting in the room she would probably say 'Oh, Harry, he wasn't that bad.' Whereupon Dad, repeating his trademark gesture of despair, would dismiss Mum's intercessions with a contemptuous comment about her lack of first-hand knowledge of some of the actor's dirtier habits. Mum, with eyes watering and bunions throbbing, would put down her knitting, pick up her library book – *Long Life, Carrot Juice and Tarot* by Gaylord Hauser – and retreat to the kitchen for a few pages of Alternative Lifestyle Philosophy, a cup of Camp coffee and a fag.

If Nana Foster was in the room she would look up from her crocheting and chastise Dad with her Durham mother-in-law's tongue, almost certainly telling him 'Why

Harold, you buggah, our George would never have spoken to me like that.'

If Nana Pegg was sitting in the room none of this would have taken place. The television would have been turned off at the first hint of an old British film, a bag of sweets passed round and a bottle of Guinness sent for. We would have sat on the floor near her feet and she would have told us stories of when Dad was small.

Most of her stories included at least one of the following – naughty boys, a bus journey or a search for 'the dog with two tails'. The naughty boys were Nana's three sons, Harold, Bill and George; the journey was any trip that Nana recalled; the dog was the distraction she invented to occupy her children during the journey to somewhere. This 'somewhere' might have been a day at the seaside, a visit to an aunt and uncle, a picnic in the country or an evening outing to a variety show. Whatever the destination or occasion, Nana must have been hard-pressed keeping her horde under control. If all the children went along there would have been the three boys plus her four daughters – Nan, Den, Eve and Rene. George, her husband, was probably working overtime at the film studios so she would have led her expeditions single-handedly.

It was during one expedition, with some of her brood growing restless on the top deck of a London trolley bus, that Nana Pegg first invited them to keep an eye open for the two-tailed creature. Dad thinks this was a cat which paraded its freak appendage from the roof of some West London villa, but I'm certain that Nana Pegg told me it was a dog. I don't know how many times the beast was spotted in pre-war London, but I revived it in pre-illness Avon when I led my own groups of children to school camps and on educational visits, promising a jam doughnut to anyone who sighted that elusive dog with two tails.

The family outing I most enjoyed hearing about was

161

the theatre visit, when Nana and company tucked into cake and sandwiches while watching an early evening show at somewhere like Shepherds Bush Empire. I don't think the picnic had to be smuggled into the auditorium by Nana, theatre managers of that time accepting that it was a common occurrence. At least it was accepted in variety halls and the less glamorous touring theatres. As far as I know, the Peggs never sat in the best Royal Circle seats of the Theatre Royal, Drury Lane, to watch Jack Hulbert and Cecily Courtnedge between mouthfuls of fish-paste sandwich and sponge cake, Nana Pegg urging Rene to keep the crumbs off her best frock.

If I could suspend an audience's disbelief and invent my own childhood theatrical excursion, mixing my experiences with those of my aunts and uncles, I would have loved to sit between Aunts Nan and Den in a party of Peggs, all of us laughing uncontrollably at Peter Butterworth's bumbling White Knight in a 'Q' Theatre Christmas Show. When we weren't laughing or wiping away tears, we'd be scoffing Aunty Eve's tomato sandwiches, Uncle Jack's Pompey buns and one of Nana Pegg's rice puddings. Such is the stuff that dreams are made on, and little dreamer's tummy aches, so I enjoyed such stuff on separate occasions and contented myself with jelly and ice cream after shows at 'Q'.

I liked visiting 'Q' Theatre, especially when there was no audience to distract me. I used to explore backstage and front-of-house, both before and after shows, but best of all I liked Saturday mornings in the workshops. It was there that my dad supervised the construction of scenery for the plays in repertory, from a simple standing set for a whodunnit to ten pantomime scenes which had to be manoeuvred in and out of the tiny prompt-side scenery dock during the course of the show.

Here, too, he sometimes built toys for us, like the rifles skilfully carved from a length of pine and given to Mike and me one Christmas. He also built us a wooden pedal car, painted blue, which survived endless collisions with gateposts and garden walls, and a wooden scooter which outlived the metal Mobo models which some children scooted along the pavements of our estate. Once he built us a roundabout, four wooden seats which ran on black rubber castors over a plywood track, and all our friends begged to be allowed a turn.

'Only if you push us first,' Julie and I told them. No negotiations, take it or leave our garden.

Later, a full-size gypsy caravan transferred from repertory at 'Q' to a long run in our back garden, and played a leading role in many of our games. It staged gunfights and epic sieges, with Billy Fox and Nigel Clegg in their Davy Crockett hats and Mike refusing to be a dead Apache. My bravest moment came when I halted the advancing Confederate army with the heroic words 'Faynites, I want to reload my gun.'

That caravan also hosted many high society dolls' tea parties, Carol Pugh delicately pouring rosehip tea into red plastic cups and Julie politely passing round jam sandwiches on yellow melamine plates. And one summer afternoon the caravan became *Emergency Ward Ten*, with Pat and Diane Taylor (aged about twelve and eleven) as doctors in charge. It was all very innocent, I recall, with none of that 'You show me your stethoscope and I'll let you see my appendix scar' stuff. However, I clearly remember standing in a long queue outside the caravan door, waiting my turn to see the doctors. Very realistic.

I often travelled to 'Q' with my dad on Saturday mornings, arriving at the scenery shop when the place was already alive with easy-paced activity. I suppose that there were deadlines to be met and an occasional crisis at 'Q', but I never witnessed there any of my dad's sudden outbursts of rage and exasperation which were always such a predictable feature of later get-ins, get-outs, fit-ups and technical rehearsals at various theatres. I'm certain that, even though the pay and conditions were not as good as those he later enjoyed elsewhere, the happiest times of Dad's working life were those spent at 'Q'.

My memories of Saturday mornings in the scenery shop are happy ones, too. I loved the smells of the place: a glue pot bubbling away over a hissing and stuttering gas ring; freshly-sized canvas and fireproofed French flats; the oily heat from the heart of an exhausted electric saw; sawdust stored in tea chests or swept into gently-sloped mountains. I also loved the noises of the place: the rattle of nails in jam jars; the skiffle of panel pins in tins, and screws in boxes; the even beat of inch-and-a-half ovals punched home in a length of 'two be one'; the high whine of a jig saw cutting across a sheet of ply; the roar of a rip saw devouring rough timber; the hoarse voice of a tenon tiptoeing carefully around the joints of a prop mirror.

At lunchtime on Saturdays we would adjourn to a Kew pub, sometimes the Star and Garter next door but usually a smaller, friendlier place overlooking the River Thames just a few minutes walk away along the towpath. While I sucked lemonade up a white waxed straw which always grew limp and useless, or searched the depths of my crisp packet for an elusive blue twist of salt, my dad downed three or more pints of bitter with his friend Peter Smith, a wholesaler from nearby Brentford market whose beer belly amply illustrated that he spent as much time ordering rounds of drinks as selling pounds of carrots. Still, the fresh air of market life, combined with as many potatoes as he liked and all the Fuller's ale he could quaff, helped to make Peter a lively companion. Surprisingly, considering his sack-of-sprouts profile, Peter was a superb ballroom dancer, nimbly sweeping around the polished floor of the Boathouse, no more than a minute's waltz away from 'Q'.

After lunch by the river, we would retrace our towpath walk, climb the steps beside Kew Bridge, cross the road and enter through the gates of Brentford market into Peter's world. It was here, one Saturday afternoon, that

I first heard an adult swear during a normal conversation. I was aged nine at the time, had occasionally heard my parents swear in anger, but only used words like 'bloody' and 'balls' myself when telling jokes or chanting playground rhymes. Although I was often in trouble, I never swore on a regular and objectionable basis until I went to grammar school. However, I was once caught by my dad when conducting a performance of a mildly risqué rhyme taught me by Fred Salisbury.

The occasion was the felling of an old and rotten oak tree which stood on the triangular green in front of our house. A large crowd of excited children and interested adults gathered to watch the event, my friends and I choosing to sit on a six-foot wall by the school gates so we might have an unobstructed view. After Brian Beasley had told a few jokes (as told to him by his sailor brother, David, and, therefore, over the heads and not between the legs of us pre-pubescent innocents) I ran through my risqué rhyme, part of which went:

Some say he died of the lergy,
Some say he died of a fit,
But I know what he died of –
That terrible smell of shhhhine your buttons with
  Brasso,
It's only three ha'pence a tin.
Buy it or nick it from Woolworth's
Whenever they've got some in.

Some say he's buried in a churchyard,
Some say he's buried in a pit,
But I know where he's buried –
Under six foot of shhhhine your buttons with Brasso,
It's only three ha'pence a tin.
Buy it or nick it from Woolworth's
Whenever they've got some in.

It was while standing up on the school wall, waving my

arms like Ralph Reader in front of a Cup Final crowd and shining buttons for all of Stafford Road, that my dad came along to move his car before the final stage of the felling operation. He didn't need to say anything to me, his presence being quite sufficient to make my voice rapidly diminish into a distant, quiet corner of Woolworth's. I thought that I would be in deep trouble but Dad, either conscious of the excitement in the air or concerned about the imminent possible collision of old oak tree with the roof of his Mini, just smiled in my direction and waved a mildly admonishing index finger at my choral group.

Fifteen minutes later a tractor belonging to the Ruislip and Northwood Urban District Council Parks Department took up the strain on a steel cable and moved at a snail's speed away from the crowd and in the direction of Barry Clegg's house; the old tree groaned, cracked loudly at the jeering children, leaned in slow motion, toppled helplessly to earth and snapped in two. It came to rest exactly where planned, midway between the privet hedges on either side of Stafford Road, most of the length of its rotten trunk on the green in front of the Andrews's house.

The adult onlookers, probably reflecting on the transient nature of life, turned sadly away and returned indoors. The children remained to watch the last rites: the old tree dismembered; limbs and trunks loaded onto the Parks Department trailer; brushwood and sawdust collected together in a pyre atop the stump of the tree, the evidence anointed with a sprinkling of petrol and publicly cremated. Viewing from our wall, Brian Beasley and I commenced our dirge:

> Shhhhine your buttons with Brasso,
> It's only three ha'pence a tin.
> Buy it or nick it from Woolworth's
> Whenever they've got some in.

Although none of my friends were angels, most of us went in for mischief rather than crime, and swearing – even by children from the most ill-disciplined homes – was not as commonplace as it is today. It was a complete revelation for me, then, while buying sprouts in Brentford market one Saturday afternoon, to hear a market porter tell my dad 'You won't get a fucking better price anywhere else, Harry . . .' Dad interrupted with 'Watch your language in front of the lad,' but the deed was done, a seed implanted in my fertile imagination. I was both fascinated and impressed by the casual use of that four-letter word, which hadn't escaped carelessly or been employed for effect but was merely another part of someone's everyday vocabulary. However, when I later tried to use my newly-acquired knowledge of English as she is spoke, in Class 3A of Ruislip Gardens Primary School, I was to discover that my teacher was neither as fascinated nor as impressed as me.

'This afternoon, just for a change, we shall attempt to do some creative writing,' said Miss Astell, my teacher. 'I want you to use your imagination and pretend that you are in one of the following three places – a circus tent, London Zoo or a busy railway station. Imagine what the people around you might be saying. They might well say "Here come the funny old clowns," or "Look at that green parrot," or "Where do I catch the train to Crewe?" Write down just one thing that you think you might hear, and then we will read out everything, one after another, so we get the impression of being in a crowd at the circus, at a zoo or in a railway station.'

Miss Astell must have recently been on a course, I realize now, but at the time I was just very happy that an English lesson was something other than writing the life story of a sixpence or copying lists of collective nouns. I chose my situation, used my imagination, wrote down my piece of background chatter, then played with my inkwell

167

while waiting for my less creative classmates to complete the exercise.

When Miss Astell thought everyone had finished, she began her flirtation with creative writing at the circus, where David Payne and six others observed the clowns:

'Look at funny old Coco!'
'Look at funny old Boppo!'
'Look at funny old Zeppo!'
'Look at funny old Coco and Boppo!'
'Look at funny old Zeppo and Coco!'
'Look at funny old Boppo and Zeppo!'
'Look at all the funny old clowns!'

Zoo time was less popular, with only Betty Sewell and Norah Hunt, Ronnie Watson and Barry Grant wandering round Regents Park – all of them looking at green parrots. The railway station was the most crowded place, with half the class asking about the same Crewe train. A few were searching for porters; Judith Walton waited in a queue at the ticket office; Pat Honour wanted directions to the public conveniences; Geoff Dyson was train-spotting with Ian Allen. Stephen Richards, school genius and destined to be at least a First Class classics degree ahead of the rest of us, read out his unique, first-class, all-time classic contribution:

'The train now arriving at Platform Nine is the 11.20 from Glasgow, a Balmoral Class 6–4–4 engine, "The Pride of Tannochbrae". British Railways is proud to announce that she is exactly three minutes and twenty-seven seconds early.'

I was surprised that he hadn't also announced the name of the train driver, together with his collar size, colour of socks, date of birth and favourite football team. My surprise, however, was abruptly prised away when Miss Astell pointed in my direction, the signal for me to follow Stephen Richards. Armed with my knowledge of Brentford market realspeak, and determined as ever to be different, my voice in the crowd shouted out crossly:

'When's that bloody train coming?'

You could have heard half a Percy Dalton peanut drop on Stephen Richards's Platform Nine; Beryl Lyons's face went so red that you couldn't see her freckles; Victor Holden nearly choked on his chewing gum; and Pat Honour almost wet herself on the spot just thinking of Miss Astell's reaction.

I now know, from my own teaching experience, that teachers are at their most unpredictable on Friday afternoons, sometimes light-headed and sweet-tempered in anticipation of the forthcoming weekend, but more often heavy-limbed and ill-tempered after the exertions of the week. Swearing, then, at 3.15 on a Friday afternoon is not to be recommended, even in these enlightened times. Swearing in 1958, at 3.15 on a Friday afternoon at the end of a week when it had rained incessantly, in the class of a spinster soon to retire on health grounds, was nothing short of a suicidal act of folly.

'What did you say?' demanded Miss Astell, with just the correct hint of controlled aggression that could only have come from over thirty years of single-minded devotion to euthanasing the spirit of little individuals like me.

'When's that bloody train coming?' I repeated brazenly.

Victor Holden coughed and swallowed his Bobo gum with an enormous gulp, Stephen Richards turned his head to gaze at me incredulously and Pat Honour raised an arm urgently.

'Yes, yes, off you go,' bellowed Miss Astell, recognizing the telltale signs of Pat's contorted legs and pleading eyes, not wanting to have to send for the caretaker, mop and bucket, last thing on a Friday.

As Pat's plimsolled feet disappeared at speed down the

corridor and into the late afternoon, the squat Mr Toad look-alike who was my teacher once again demanded 'What did you say?' I repeated my response, almost as boldly as before. Miss Astell's eyes went bloodshot behind her pebble-lensed spectacles. Advancing menacingly towards me between two rows of desks, she swiped a glancing blow to Paul Butler's skull with her *First Aid in English* and firmly but politely asked dear Stephen Richards to turn around and face the front. She avoided David Barker's accidentally-on-purpose-left-out left leg, commanded me to stand up and confronted me nose to nose, eyeball to spectacle, her hand-knitted mauve cardigan only inches away from my trembling heart. The demolition of my spirit was about to commence, each of her words delivered slowly and deliberately, sprayed and spat, three parts malevolence to one part Paraquat.

'So you like to swear, Stephen Pegg? You imagine that's the sort of language you would hear at a railway station?'

I nodded my head twice, defiantly.

'I suppose you think a normal, decent person would talk like that, do you?'

I nodded once more.

'Well, if you like to use that sort of filthy language, please carry on. Say it again.'

I said it again.

'And once again,' she said.

Once again I said it.

'Again,' she ordered.

And again I obeyed.

Miss Astell dabbed at her forehead with a pretty pink embroidered handkerchief, crushed a butterfly and two cornflowers between a thumb and some fingers. By now she was salivating grotesquely, growing slowly more angry and gradually losing control. But the confidence I'd had amongst the crowd on Platform Nine just minutes earlier also began to drift away as she metamorphosed three inches from my nose, from eccentric Mr Toad into slavering Willoughby Goddard, Gessler the interrogator to my captive William Tell.

'So, Stephen Pegg, you clever little cynic,
if you like to use that sort of disgusting language
[Lesley Uttin, fetch me those thumbscrews]
you can talk like that until you get fed up
with the sound of such foul-mouthed filth.
[Paul McDuell, heat the branding-irons]
And, allow me to explain to any of your smutty
    little friends
who might be smirking behind their grubby little
    hands that
[Julia Knowles, prepare the rack immediately]
no-one leaves this room until you
learn how to speak properly,
without using that nasty little word.
[Robert Ash, send for my hangman]
I hope you all understand that.'

William Tell, even with wrists and ankles chained, cross-bow confiscated and a Cox's Orange Pippin stuffed in his gob, would have effected a successful escape from that evil overlord Gessler. I was confronted by a force more dreadful than anything dreamed up by ATV's scriptwriters, though, Miss Willoughby Toad-Astell in full flight on a Friday afternoon.

Bravely as I tried, after asking 'When's that bloody train coming?' a dozen times under Herr Gessler's laser gaze, my resolve weakened and I began to cry, slowly at first but by the time I had capitulated and compliantly enquired 'When's that train coming?' my tears were blinding me.

'That's much better,' said the leering Willoughby Goddard.

The minute hand on the classroom clock limped

towards the six, signalling end of resistance, end of confrontation, end of lesson, end of week, end of me.

'Much better,' agreed Mr Toad triumphantly.

Outside the headmaster's office the school secretary checked the time by her H. Samuel Everite and rang the bell. Our classroom door burst open.

'Where have you been all this time, Patricia Honour?' asked Miss Astell. 'Oh, never mind. Everyone stand up quietly. Stephen Richards, lead your row out first. Not you, Stephen Pegg! You can wait until everyone else has gone.'

As everyone else filed out I wiped my eyes with my shirt cuffs and avoided looking at any of my friends, ashamed that I'd wept in front of them. Miss Astell tidied her desk, blew her nose, locked away her pens and pencils.

'You may go now,' she announced without looking up, dropping her keys into the depths of her handbag. I walked quickly from my classroom and along the silent, childless corridor, past the house points board and permanently displayed Shell Countryside posters, down the staircase, between the Infants' assembly hall and library area, out through the exit doors and into the real world.

Just two minutes later I was locked inside our downstairs lavatory, standing on the toilet seat and staring out of the window.

I watched Miss Astell as she collected her bicycle from the caretaker's dustbin enclosure above the boiler room and behind the coke pile.

She swapped a few words with blue-dungareed Mr Baxter, the assistant caretaker.

He held open a gate as she wheeled her bicycle out.

The gate squealed shut.

Miss Astell placed her handbag in the basket attached to the handlebars of her bike.

She adjusted her skirt and spectacles and wished Mr Baxter good night.

She scooted down the sloping school driveway, climbed astride her saddle and cycled off in the direction of her weekend. As I observed all this I was using my imagination.

'Now, I want you to imagine that you are following a cyclist along a quiet country lane when she gets stuck on a level crossing, the front wheel of her bike jams in the track and her skirt becomes tangled with the bicycle chain. The gates of the crossing are down. The level-crossing keeper hasn't noticed the cyclist because he's busy feeding his green parrot. How would you attract his attention? What would you shout to him?'

'When's that bloody train coming?'

'Q' Theatre and the area near Kew Bridge hold many happy memories for me. Years later, long after the theatre had been demolished and an office block built on its site, I still enjoyed going there. Ros was at college, just a little higher up the river at Twickenham, and on Sundays we often walked along the towpath to Kew, watching the boats and birds on the Thames, stopping at a riverside pub for lunch, staring enviously into other people's houses and gardens.

'Q' was an intimate little theatre with a small stage and auditorium. At least, that is how I remember it and, compared to the Piccadilly, the Lyceum, the Festival Hall and other places where I later worked, 'Q' was minute. It was its very intimacy which, I suppose, held the key to the strange nervous condition which first afflicted me when I began theatre-going there in the fifties and wasn't cured until I stood up, clapped my hands and stamped my feet in time to the exuberant singing of the *Black Nativity* company at the Piccadilly in 1960.

I was always a shy little boy, and not much better

when I got bigger. One of my earliest memories is of hiding under the dining-table when Harry and Florrie Robinson (Julie's godparents) came from Catford for tea one Sunday. I stayed there until they left. I did grow out of hiding under tables but was never blessed with too much self-confidence. Strange, then, that I later chose to teach and be a football referee. Not for nothing was I forever singing to myself 'Hi diddley dee, an actor's life for me.'

My shyness manifested itself at 'Q' whenever I stood for the National Anthem before a show began. At that time, I thought that my dad was the most famous man in Kew and Ruislip. It seemed to me that everyone knew Harry Pegg, and all the world wanted to say hallo to him. I was convinced that every member of every 'Q' audience knew that my dad had built the scenery, where he sat and who sat with him. When we stood for The Queen, therefore, I was convinced that almost everyone else in the auditorium was looking at us, and as I felt hundreds of eyes staring at me, my ears grew hot and red. And the hotter and redder they got, the more attention they attracted. And the more gazers I imagined to be gazing at my embarrassment, the sillier I felt.

Eventually, growing tired of the burden of my own shyness, I developed a strategy which I hoped would explain away my acute discomfort to all those who stared at me. Pretending that I had something in my eye, a speck of dust or an eyelash, I would poke it with a finger and rub it with a knuckle. Then I would tug at Dad's jacket and complain about the soreness of my eye, and he would gently hold my infant head in his huge hands and gently turn it towards the chandelier above us in order that he might detect and remove the offending mote. The gazers would then know why my ears had glowed like coals and whisper understandingly to each other.

Just then the National Anthem would end and the house lights fade. We sat down, the front tabs rose, Dad's set was revealed and the first line spoken. 'I'll be all right,' I'd whisper, rubbing my eye once more for effect and relaxing back into my seat to make the most of the anonymity of the dark.

QQQQQQQQQQ

After 'Q', Dad went to work at Stage Decor scenery constructors in Walworth, not far from the Elephant and Castle and the Old Kent Road. If Kew and Brentford Market seemed exciting to nine-year-old me, the Walworth area made them appear genteel and tame by comparison. Throughout history Kew must have always been a popular place in which to live. Being so near to the river and Royal parks, as it grew from country village to Greater London jigsaw piece it had probably always attracted the affluent and upwardly mobile. Walworth, however, was a part of London which might once have been fashionable, but was now run-down and rough, its untidy terraced streets and impersonal system-built tower blocks housing some of the capital's most disadvantaged citizens. It was an interesting and lively place, though, and all the people I met there were kind and friendly.

I earned pocket money at Stage Decor at weekends and in school holidays by brushing up sawdust and sorting out loose screws, sizing and glueing scenery, loading and unloading the lorries, making tea and buying cakes. I even helped to paint backcloths under the guidance of Hubert Gregg, an eccentric and bearded Austrian scenic artist.

Hubert drove to work from his home in St John's Wood in a three-wheeled Messerschmitt car, a sight which caused much amusement amongst the carpenters, prop-makers and other scenic artists. When my dad, for some obscure reason, exchanged his trusty Bond Minicar

175

for a Heinkel bubblecar, he too became the butt of the workshop comedians, inspiring many jokes with a Nazi reference. Even Hubert joined in, drawing a cartoon of Herr Pegg blitzkrieging St John's Wood in a Heinkel dive-bomber, paint tins and brushes flying through the sky following a direct hit on the Gregg residence.

Sometimes, when there were no jobs for me at Stage Decor, Dad dropped me off at the Imperial War Museum in Kennington and I spent a few hours wandering amongst the exhibits. I particularly liked the models depicting trench warfare because I could switch on tiny lights and see networks of tunnels. The underground holes in which soldiers lived looked so cosy and exciting in those models, just like something from *Wind in the Willows* I always thought. It never once registered on my innocent mind that soldiers lived AND died in those underground holes. Somehow I don't think the Imperial War Museum was telling the truth about military conflict. Not to me, at least.

Stage Decor was housed in an old Quaker meeting place, Robert Browning Hall. Scenery was constructed in the main body of the hall, and the offices were upstairs in what had been the gallery. The pulpit and a few wall plaques were still in place but hidden beneath layers of sawdust, inscriptions and dates only just legible. The ceiling plaster was cracked and flaking, precariously held in place by a thousand and one spiders' webs.

Robert Browning Hall was situated at one end of East Street Market, the end furthest from Walworth Road. Not far from the hall, on the opposite side of the road, was a fish and chip shop where I'd sometimes buy myself lunch, even when Mum had made me sandwiches. In the market my dad bought fruit and vegetables from a stall run by the wife of Stan Davis, another carpenter who worked at Stage Decor. At Christmastime we snapped up cheap crackers, picked dates and selected nuts from other stallholders. On the Walworth Road Dad bought himself suits and me a donkey jacket, from one of the many tailors and outfitters there, all of them seemingly run by different members of the same Jewish family.

Apart from the fish and chip shop and market stalls near Robert Browning Hall, food figures in a few more Walworth memories. Not far away was a seafood stall, selling things like cockles, winkles, whelks and shrimps. I'd seen them all before, and eaten most at home on Sundays or somewhere along the seafront at Southend, but it was in Walworth that I first sampled jellied eels, just one tiny mouthful from a large bowl that my dad consumed with much enthusiasm. Well, he may have enjoyed them, but I certainly didn't. I can safely claim to have been an unfussy, adventurous eater all my life, but I doubt whether I could ever learn to love jellied eels. I loathed equally the texture of fish and taste of jelly, and regurgitating eel vertebrae into the palm of my hand after struggling to swallow flesh and jelly seemed to me an appropriate conclusion to the whole experience.

One lunchtime Dad introduced me to the pleasures of an East End pie and eel shop. The one we visited was just like a fish and chips restaurant except neither fish nor chips were on offer. The menu choice was between meat pie and jellied eels, so you don't get any prizes for guessing my choice. To go with my individual meat pie there was mashed potato and 'liquor', special gravy made to a secret recipe. Each pie and eel shop family had its own recipe, traditionally handed down from generation to generation. The pies were probably made to a closely-guarded secret recipe, too, every family adding their own this, that and the other. Unfortunately for me, the other secret ingredient in my particular pie was a black beetle. It wasn't huge but it was, nevertheless, an unpleasant surprise, floating on its back amongst the traditional this and that. I didn't have my 'I-Spy Pies' book on me so I wouldn't have been able to identify my secret ingredient, but when Dad took my plate back to the counter I felt sure I heard him say 'cockroach'. I don't know who else heard him, but the proprietor didn't want it repeated and Dad was immediately placated with the promise of free lunch. The knowledge that our food wouldn't cost anything made Dad tuck in with even greater enthusiasm than was normal. I was given another meal but I kept seeing that beetle on its back so the thought of cutting into my pie was mental torture. I ate my mash and liquor but Dad wolfed the pie.

On another day when I was helping at Stage Decor my dad took me for lunch in a local fish restaurant. Now this was not one of your expensive and trendy bistros with its extensive

MENU GASTRONOMIQUE

****

Poached Sea Bass

Kiwi Fruit and Brill

Gravadlax

Krill

Julienne of Porpoise

Fruits de Mer in Cream

Starfish à la mode de Calvados

Assiette vide de
nouvelle cuisine

****

This was more like the back room behind the fryers in your typical friendly fish and chip shop. From a tiny elevated corner shelf a framed photograph of the Queen Mother surveyed the room: a trio of brent geese migrated across a recently-painted, blue gloss (eggshell finish) sky; half a dozen different patterns of wallpaper fought on the other walls; a mix-and-match linoleum floor curled beneath brown bentwood chairs and checked plastic tablecloths; a cruet set and sauce bottle stood near the centre of every second table. The place was busy and crowded, bright and clean, with more sounds and smells than wallpaper patterns: the cutting of crisp cod, chomping of chips; salt sprinkled over warm vinegar; the clash of battle between fork and plate; Count Dracula's nephews crawling under tables and around legs, chips for fangs and red sauce on chins; the stirring of spoon in cup; an occasional slurp, a sigh.

Finding a just-vacated table, we sat down and I tidied four sets of debris into one pile within reach of Alma Cogan's younger sister, the industrious teenage waitress buzzing between kitchen, shop and dining room with several plates and the promise of 'Wivyou innermo', darlin'.' My dad, never the most patient man, endured three 'wivyou inners' and just two 'mo's' before standing up and steaming into the shop to have a word with the man doing all the frying. I watched their one-sided conversation, my dad waving arms in all directions – at me, young Miss Cogan, the geese, the Queen Mother – while the fish fryer calmly scooped chips from an angry vat of bubbling fat. Eventually, Dad beckoned me over, introduced me to his friend the fryer and invited me to select my meal from the menu chalked on a board behind the counter and above shelves of assorted bottles and jars. There were bottles of red sauce, brown sauce and vinegar; jars of pickled onions, pickled eggs, pickled cabbage and pickled gherkins; and enough bottles of pop to rot all the teeth in Walworth, twice!

JARS OF PICKLED ONIONS·BOTTLES OF MALT
VINEGAR·JARS OF PICKLED EGGS·BOTTLES
OF RED SAUCE·JARS OF PICKLED GHERKINS·
BOTTLES OF BROWN SAUCE·CHERRYADE !
POP ! LEMONADE ! POP ! POP ! LIMEADE !
POP ! ORANGEADE ! DANDELION AND BUR-
DOCK ! POP ! GINGER BEER ! POP ! ICE CREAM
SODA ! COLA ! POP ! (ROTS YOUR TEETH)
COLA (ROTS YOUR TEETH) ! POP ! COLA

The graphic impact of the chalk scrawl was much less
appealing than the hypnotic chorus line of sauce, pop
and pickle, but I chose cod fillet, chips and peas, and a
cup of tea.

'Got that, John?' Dad asked his friend. 'And I'll have
a large plaice, large chips, large peas, bread and butter
and a mug of tea, please. Better make that double bread,
John, the lad'll probably want some.'

We returned to our table and John conveyed our order
to his waitress.

'Sorry, love,' my dad said to her when she brought two
piled plates and placed them before us, 'but we've only
got half an hour for lunch.'

She looked at the large plaice, large chips, large peas
and double portion of bread and butter set before my dad,
looked at him, looked once more at his plate, looked at
him again.

'That's all right, darlin',' was all she said, glancing one

last double portion look of incredulity at his fully-laden plate before recommencing her buzz between tables, shop and kitchen.

Fish and chips is a much-underestimated British contribution to world gastronomy, but the best fish and chips bear comparison with any food that I've sampled in other parts of the globe. I have tasted excellent fish and chips – both on a plate and out of paper – in many English and Welsh towns, the very best meal I've ever eaten coming from a tiny restaurant near Kessingland in Suffolk. That meal was enjoyed in the summer of 1969 with Ros and our friends Malcolm and Carolyn, and the bill for all four of us came to 17/6d (about 90p) including bread and butter and a cup of tea.

John's Walworth platter was good enough to join Kessingland in my all-time Top Ten, scoring highly for both quantity and quality. Unfortunately, I was tucking into my meal with such enthusiasm that I failed to notice a rogue bone lurking in the fillet upon my plate, and consumed it along with a mouthful of more nutritious fayre. Cod and chips, bread and peas all negotiated my mouth and throat and set off for my stomach, but the bone stopped halfway down my throat and lodged itself there to protest painfully on behalf of Fishes' Rights Groups everywhere.

'Dad,' I croaked, going red in the face, 'I've swallowed a bone.'

'That cod was filleted,' he asserted. 'Are you sure?'

I nodded my head.

'Where's it stuck?' he asked.

I pointed at my throat, just beginning to panic as breathing became difficult. John was summoned, ceased scooping, rushed over.

'Whassamatter, Aitch? Bone stuck, izzit? Yeah, Aitch I know that. 'Course, 'course. 'Course youright, Aitch, butitjustaintpossible togetallthembonesout, me old mate.

181

Yeah, yeah. I know, I know. I knowitsays "fillet" on the board, but . . .'

I really wasn't too worried about misleading descriptions or apportioning blame, being by now acutely concerned about my diminishing oxygen supply and the size of the crowd attracted by my loud impersonation of a moose on heat. Some of my audience shouted advice to John and Dad – 'Turnim upsidedown!' 'Slapimardonizback!' – 'Ring for an ambulance!' – 'Get a torch!' – 'Put yer fingers downiz froat!' 'Take the money!' – 'Open the box!' – until the crowd grew suddenly silent upon the arrival of Alma's sister. She waved the thick crusty corner of a loaf of bread underneath my dad's nose.

'Try this, darlin'. Do the trick in arfermo'.'

Then off she buzzed. The crust was thrust into my moose mouth and I chewed and gasped, chewed and gasped

chew – chew – gasp – gasp – chew

until the bread and bone and crowd were gone. John removed the remains of my meal, the chips and peas now cold and congealed beside the offending cod fillet, and returned a little later with a replacement dish.

'There you are, son. No expense spared. Plaice, same as yer farver. No bleedin' bones in that, Aitch!'

In 1960 Dad moved to the Piccadilly Theatre in Denman Street, in the heart of the West End. Wandering around Walworth and the Imperial War Museum would henceforth be replaced by exploration of the streets and attractions of central London. The Piccadilly was one of four theatres owned by the Albery family, the others being the Criterion, Wyndham's and the New (later renamed the Albery). Julie's godfather, Harry Robinson, was master carpenter at the New and was probably responsible for getting Dad to move from Stage Decor. When Harry retired about ten years later Dad succeeded him as chief carpenter of the Albery group.

The show running at the Piccadilly when Dad took charge was *The Amorous Prawn*, described on the posters outside the theatre as 'the new laughter hit by Anthony Kimmins'. It had already been on for about a year and would stay for another twelve months, giving Dad some time to get his bearings and begin to make changes. One of the first things he did was sort out an untidy sink area near the prompt corner. Well, to be completely accurate, it was one of the first things he gave me to do.

That sink area was where Pat Mooney, one of the daymen, prepared the prop drinks for the show. Whisky was concocted from water and gravy browning and put into an empty Haig bottle, while the gin was made by filling a Gordon's bottle with tap water. Although only two bottles were used in the show, Pat kept several dozen more on a window ledge above the sink. I don't know if they were Pat's own empties, himself being fond of a drop of the hard stuff, to be sure, but all they did was gather dust. I disposed of most of those bottles, keeping just a few as standby props. I was also asked to clean the sink, but I very quickly decided that it was impossible for me single-handedly to remove decades of abuse with some Vim and a scouring pad so I used to watch understudy rehearsals instead. When Dad caught me waiting in the wings he soon found me another job, away from the distractions of actors and ASMs.

My next task was probably the least mentally demanding I did during a dozen years at the Piccadilly. I had to polish all the front-of-house stair rods, every brass rod from every staircase that led from the foyer of the theatre. This amounted to a whole lot of rods. I used to remove them in threes and fours, take them to the workshop deep in the bowels of the backstage area and polish. I polished for three hours each Saturday morning and I polished all through the summer of 1960. On Saturday mornings I polished in the workshop, listening to stage sounds from the Tannoy above my head, and that summer I polished

183

in the staff room, sitting with a stair rod between my legs while watching Test match cricket in flickering black and white. Although polishing was a tedious occupation I, nevertheless, felt proud whenever I walked up and down the Piccadilly's staircases and admired my handiwork. I had only just finished polishing my way down to the Stalls Bar and up to the Upper Circle offices when Ian Albery decided to replace all the staircase carpet, together with all my brass rods. I was not a happy lad.

The star of *Amorous Prawn* was Evelyn Laye, an actress who had appeared in the very first show at the Piccadilly in 1920 something, *Blue Eyes*. During the run of *Amorous Prawn* Miss Laye celebrated her sixtieth birthday, and I remember sitting in the front row of the stalls one morning to watch Richard Baker, then a well-known newsreader, interview her for a regional news magazine programme. He also spoke to me, but our brief conversation wasn't on television the following evening.

After *The Amorous Prawn* closed there were lots of short-lived shows at the Piccadilly. Their failure was bad news for people who had invested money in them, and it was definitely bad news for the members of each company every time 'the notice went up'. This harmless-sounding phrase meant that the company manager had pinned to a board near the stage door a brief formal announcement of the show's impending death. 'Angel Theatre Ltd regrets that the final performance of *Man From The Market* will be on . . .' Bad news for company members, however, was good news for my dad. It almost always led to him working long hours, first on the get-out of the failed show and then on the get-in of a new show, and long hours equalled large pay packets. Some people may have shed genuine tears when the notice went up but Dad just cried all the way to the Midland Bank, Walworth Road branch.

I can't remember the names of those flops, and the only one I recall seeing starred Robert Morley and Cleo

Laine. I think that particular show ran for just eight performances. At about this time I used to watch many 'limited season' productions at the Piccadilly, notably *Black Nativity* and Marcel Marceau. Both made several return visits to the theatre, 'back by popular demand' the billboards shouted. This was definitely an honest claim for the French mime but may have been a little less than the gospel truth as far as the American show was concerned. It didn't make economic sense for the building to remain empty for long periods between shows so sometimes a stopgap was put on to prevent the theatre being dark. I'm certain that *Black Nativity* occasionally returned by management demand.

I spent a lot of my free time at the Piccadilly doing odd jobs to earn myself pocket money, but I didn't work as a showman until *The Masters* in 1962. Showmen were part-time workers, employed to move scenery and props during a show. Whenever possible a theatre's master carpenter employed showmen who could work every evening performance plus both matinées, but 'eight-show men' were rare so there was always plenty of extra work available on matinée days. Workers from other theatres, like Harry Butlin, master carpenter at Her Majesty's, and John Wallbank from Wyndham's frequently used to help Dad on their free afternoons, I remember.

Most matinées, especially when a show needed a lot of showmen, were frantic occasions. *The Masters* was just such a show because it had two quick changes involving the setting and striking of a banquet table. Most of Dad's showmen had jobs outside the theatre which prevented them from doing the midweek matinée so I was called upon to help. I think that I informed my school of a series of hospital appointments, so while my classmates spent Wednesday afternoons conjugating French verbs and watching litmus paper change colour I rushed onstage to strike a chair and two claret glasses.

A stage manager always supervised those changes with a stopwatch in his hand, informing Dad of 'our time' once the house tabs had gone up. Wednesday matinée times weren't ever as good as evening performances, our stage crew forever short of performers.

I remember that quite a lot of 'eight-show men' worked at Covent Garden market, the early start and finish to their working day enabling them to earn extra money in the West End if they wished. By the time the market had moved to Nine Elms, in about 1970, I don't think we had any market workers doing shows at the Piccadilly. Once the journey to the West End became longer than the walk from Covent Garden I guess that most of them gave up their double life.

I was always well-treated by the other showmen. In some cases this was because I was the master carpenter's son, but for the majority I was just a youngster they wanted to befriend. Some of the market porters used to bring me bags of fruit; one man, a teacher in a private school, gave me some books which he thought I'd enjoy; a Scots flyman attempted to teach me how to play chess; and when I grew tall and looked old enough to take to the pub I went for a drink with some of them.

Nearly all West End pubs were then uninviting places. Those near the theatre seemed even less inviting than the rest. However, I used to go to one close by with Dad for a tasty lunch in the upstairs dining room, but a couple of half-pints of lager and lime with the showmen tasted even better.

When George, the publican, closed his dining room and replaced tasty lunches with bar snacks the place became even less inviting but, curiously, a little more interesting. This was entirely due to the hotplate that was installed on one end of the bar. This hotplate occasionally bore a cottage pie or a cheese and tomato flan, but on at least twenty-seven days of each month of the year it used to carry a Pyrex dish of sausages. I'm certain that some of these sausages made an appearance on the first day of each month and were still performing at least twenty-six days later. Just like the nudes at the nearby Windmill Theatre, they never moved.

Despite his knowledge of their history, and constant warnings from Mum about the dangers of 'buying sausages out', my dad was forever eating them. The hotplate was placed at the end of the bar most favoured by the Piccadilly stage crew, the end nearest the door. This end was favoured for enabling a thirsty stagehand to order a swift pint during the interval and then make an even swifter exit to be on stage in time for the next change. This soon became the end where Dad would lean with his back to George, spike a warm sausage with a wooden cocktail stick and consume it in just a couple of quick mouthfuls. I always cringed with embarrassment, convinced that George would catch Dad and eject us from the pub. Upon reflection, George probably knew what was happening in front of Dad's back and allowed him to play Russian roulette with those sausages, Dad being such a regular customer that it would have been folly for George to ban him. I'm surprised that my dad never succumbed to a bout of serious food poisoning, though. Perhaps he avoided that by heeding Mum's advice about 'buying sausages out'. After all, he never bought them, did he?

In November 1987 I went into a pub for the last time. I was with my younger brother Ken. There is a ten-year gap between us so Ken does not feature in my early memories but we have become closer in recent years and he has been a great help since I have been ill. On this occasion, we had been to see *Blues in the Night* at the Piccadilly, and had arranged to meet Dad's successor as master carpenter for a drink during the interval. Needless to say, we met in the same old pub. Some things hadn't changed – noise, smoke, slow service – but George and the sausages had moved on. I fancied a half of lager and lime, just for old time's sake, but Ken bought me a pint of bitter. Nevertheless, I was still reminded of all my days and nights at the Piccadilly as I shakily raised a full glass with my weakening left arm. It felt just like lifting a stage weight.

The next show I recall working on was *Enrico*, a musical about Italy from 1863 to 1963 as seen through the eyes of a hundred-year-old man. *Enrico* had the largest cast of any show at the Piccadilly during Dad's time there, with more than a hundred in the company. The band room, where musicians normally prepared themselves and their instruments, became a dressing room for half a dozen male dancers, and the under-stage area had to be tidied and used as a band room.

'Just don't bend over in front of a male dancer,' was my dad's alarming advice to me when the wardrobe mistress asked him if I could help her for a fortnight. She was responsible for appointing dressers, and with a large number of musicals running in the West End at that time experienced dressers were scarce. If experienced dressers weren't available, I suppose that an inexperienced fifteen-year-old schoolboy was as good an alternative as she might expect to get, and so I found myself in the band room with half a dozen male dancers.

When my Aunty Eve came to see the show she wanted to know how I got on with them since, as she so delightfully put it, 'They looked like lovely boys.' I got on with them very well. I had to make sure their costumes were ready when they came off stage, and help them to dress whenever a quick change was called for. Despite my dad's fears none of the lovely boys in the band room made any sort of undesirable advance in my direction. They were all too much in love with themselves to bother with a spotty-faced adolescent, anyway. I have some original posters to remind me of my fortnight with those dancers. On one *Enrico* is described as 'A NEW GAY GLAMOUR MUSICAL'!

During my years in many theatres I met and worked with plenty of homosexuals, yet only one made a pass. I was a relief stage doorman at the time, and the show at the Piccadilly was a successful musical. One of the company loaned me his copy of *Last Exit to Brooklyn*, a contemporary American gay novel, and later suggested that we discuss its literary qualities in his dressing room. I declined the offer. Some years later he was found murdered in his London flat and sordid rumours appeared in some newspapers. Neither the speculation about his life nor the manner of his death much surprised me.

What I really wanted to be offered was seduction by an actress or female dancer, but the only ones that glanced in my direction were not the ones I fancied. In *Oliver* two ladies in the company made it obvious that they wanted me to consider myself well in, consider myself part of their furniture. One was sixteen, plump and Jewish, and the other was thirty, smoked and had a reputation for promiscuity. I have nothing against teenage girls, plump people or Jews but that particular combination didn't appeal to me. I have nothing against thirty-year-old women, either, and in 1967 promiscuity seemed harmless enough, but the smoker's pong was so strong I had to tell her 'It's clear we're not going to get along.'

One of the strangest shows I worked on was *Oh Dad, Poor Dad! Ma's Hung You in the Closet and I'm Feeling So Sad!* This was a black comedy by Arthur Kopit, an American writer. The stars of the production at the Piccadilly were a carnivorous plant and an actress who was almost seventy. Guess which took a shine to me? Her name was Hermione Gingold, and Dad joked that she had a reputation not unlike the Venus Flytrap which she constantly sought to upstage. Miss Gingold was one of those theatrical persons who is revered because of past success, their present failures conveniently ignored. During the thirties and forties she'd been a star of English

189

intimate revue. After the Second World War she went to America, made films in Hollywood, and was now returning to the London stage. An elderly lady I used to visit at the time was most impressed when I told her I was working with Hermione Gingold, much more impressed than when I later mentioned the names of Ian McKellen, Sarah Miles and Peter O'Toole.

Dad and the other backstage workers joked about Miss Gingold and me because it seemed as if I was the only man on stage she didn't snap at. I had to open and close a door for her in one scene, looking through a tiny hole in the scenery to await her cue. None of the showmen who had done this before me had been able to satisfy her, and all of them incurred her wrath nightly. On my matinée days, however, she couldn't have been kinder.

'When I smile at you, darling, that's your cue to open the door for me. Timing is so important, darling,' she said, tilting her head slightly and raising one eyebrow as she delivered a grin that was almost certainly wicked. When I wasn't 'darling' I was her 'young man', much to the amusement of everyone else on stage. Before I became a toy boy, though, the house tabs came down on *Oh Dad*. It didn't long survive the poor reviews it received, the notice went up, Miss Gingold gave me a final wicked grin and returned to being an English star in America.

7 August 1990: As a postscript to this short scene, I was resting on the bed yesterday afternoon when Ros plugged me in to my radio. Someone who'd recently written Hermione Gingold's biography was talking about her. It seems that at about the time I was sharing a few words and wicked grins with Miss Gingold one of her sons had suddenly become ill and died. His name was Stephen.

I always liked working on musicals. Although they were usually difficult to get-in, fit-up, rehearse and run, they always generated so much more excitement and expectation inside the theatre than a straight play. However, one play proved to be an exhilarating exception to this.

In the summer of 1965 *Ride a Cock Horse*, written by David Mercer, came into the Piccadilly for a limited season. The play wasn't particularly good or different, and didn't earn much praise from the critics, but every performance was a sell-out. This was entirely due to the one man in the cast, Peter O'Toole. He'd not appeared on the stage for quite a few years, having become a rich and famous film star after his portrayal of T. E. Lawrence in David Lean's film, *Lawrence of Arabia*. His fans ignored the play's poor notices and besieged the box office for tickets, any sort of ticket for any performance. And after all performances some fans flocked to the stage door, in a vain attempt to see their idol. They couldn't have glimpsed him very often because he usually remained in his dressing room until way past midnight, sharing the contents of a generously-stocked bar with a few friends.

I never joined Peter O'Toole for an after-show drink in dressing room number one, but I can honestly boast that every Thursday night during the run of *Ride a Cock Horse* I had a beer with him in the Queen's Head. This boast, like many things in the theatrical world, is not as impressive as it seems. When Peter O'Toole found out from my dad that the stage crew got paid on Friday, he very generously offered to pay for one drink for each stagehand every Thursday, the day when most of us would probably be skint and unable to buy ourselves a pint. I suppose that he would have loved to share a few beers with us in the Queen's Head, but fame prevented him from enjoying his fortune in so ordinary a way.

Jon Laurimore, the actor who understudied Peter O'Toole, often sat in the pub with us. He had an unenviable job, I always thought, having to learn an enormous part knowing that if he ever made an appearance most of the audience, who were only interested in seeing Peter O'Toole, would probably demand a refund of their ticket money. Jon went on just once, when Peter O'Toole was suddenly taken ill in his dressing room and was too unwell to appear in a midweek matinée. Sure enough, there were as many people queuing outside the box office for refunds as there were in the auditorium watching Jon.

Dad occasionally joined Peter O'Toole for an after-show drink. When this happened I either went home on the Underground or waited for Dad. If I had any money, and if I felt I could stand the cigarette smoke, I'd join some stagehands in the Queen's Head, but sometimes I sat in Dad's office and attempted to catch up with my 'A'-level reading. This was never easy since Peter O'Toole's dressing room was immediately above my head and the sounds of generously-stocked friends were easier on my weary intellect than Hardy or Eliot. Eventually Dad came to get me and we'd drive back to Ruislip, stopping at a restaurant if we were hungry and if it wasn't too late.

Before Westway was built we usually drove home along the Bayswater Road to Shepherd's Bush, through Acton and then down the Western Avenue. There were plenty of alternative routes if the traffic jammed, Dad knowing his way around most of London as well as any taxi driver, but the journey via Acton was favourite because it took us past three restaurants we enjoyed visiting.

Two places we liked were quite close together in Holland Park. One we'd regularly stop at was a Greek-owned restaurant which served excellent spit-roast chicken and home-made coleslaw at a very reasonable price. In Addison Avenue, just off the Bayswater Road, was Chez Moi, a more expensive place than those we normally frequented, but we liked the way they served cauliflower in a cheese sauce. This suppertime extravagance ceased with the opening of Westway, although I went there once again, in 1969, to celebrate my 21st birthday with Ros and two other friends, Rob Schofield and Ann Crane. Rob's birthday was two days before mine, neither of us wanted the fuss of a party, so we chose to take our girlfriends to Chez Moi.

I remember that Rob chose a tournedos steak and I chose the wine. Rob is now director of an American hotel group and, therefore, well able to select a good steak, but in 1969 he didn't know a tournedos from a tureen of tripe. While the rest of us congratulated ourselves on our menu selection, Rob watched in embarrassed horror as his steak turned up alone and little in the centre of a large plate. I wonder if Rob ever again ordered a tournedos steak after that gastronomic surprise.

I am now director of my own silent movies but in 1969 I had plenty to say for myself. I can no longer claim to know a lot about wine but in 1969 I had been in (and out of) the wine trade. I had passed wine examinations and attended wine tastings. Wine and me were like that, so when I ordered a young Beaujolais I asked the waiter to chill it.

'Not a red wine, sir,' he protested.

'If it's good enough for the French, then it's good enough for me. Please bring us an ice bucket,' I asserted myself while the girlfriends pretended to be invisible. I wonder if either of them ever went to a restaurant and dared to ask for a young Beaujolais to be chilled.

At the Savoy circle, East Acton was my favourite fish and chip shop, Burrows. It was run by Bob Burrows, who had been to the same school as my dad, and his wife, Pearl. Bob's mother still did all the frying on an ancient coke-fired range, even though she must have been well into her seventies. As we approached Burrows I looked for the illuminated sign on the roof of the shop. It wasn't on whenever Dad stayed for a drink with Peter O'Toole but its beacon was there most nights, as reassuring to me as a lighthouse to a mariner. Because we got there very late, sometimes all the fish and/or chips had gone, which disappointed me. More often, though, Bob or Pearl gave us extra fish and chips, at a much reduced price, which always pleased Dad.

In 1964 a musical called *Instant Marriage* ran for almost a whole year, and remains memorable for several reasons. Part of the run coincided with my summer holiday so Dad gave me a dayman's job for a month. I joined the union, NATKE, worked hard and received a very welcome wage packet every Friday.

Instant Marriage was about a West End marriage bureau run by an outrageously camp couple played by a couple of outrageously camp actors, Wallas Eaton and Tony Holland. Other characters were four unsophisticated North Country folk on holiday in London (played by Patsy Rowlands, Bob Grant, Harold Goodwin and Paul Whitson-Jones) and three strippers from a striptease club. You can probably guess another reason for *Instant Marriage* being memorable. Yes, it was those four naive North Country folk.

There were four or five different sets in *Instant Marriage*, and several scene changes which had to be done during the show. The sets were on 'trucks' which were moved into position on a revolve. One of the sets was supposed to be an expensive restaurant, upon which the hapless North Country folk stumbled during their stay in London. Having only wanted a cup of tea and a place to rest their aching feet, they were tricked by a dishonest waiter into ordering steak and champagne. Neither steak nor champagne was genuine, alas, otherwise they'd certainly have become perks.

Perks were anything in a show which someone, usually my dad, could use. In *Amorous Prawn* there had been bottles of tonic water and bitter lemon which were needed as props. A few regularly found their way into Dad's office, to be consumed by me whenever I hadn't sufficient funds to buy myself a cola in a nearby cafe. The champagne from *Instant Marriage* was a sort of perk, I suppose. It was really a charmless little ginger ale 'ordinaire', specially bottled by Schweppes and labelled to look like vintage Moët et Chandon. Nevertheless, the odd bottle was enjoyed at home, Dad joking that it was the real thing until the cork came out without the characteristic explosive force. Pops often went missing on stage, too, the actor who played the restaurant waiter always improvising an implausible excuse for the gullible Northerners.

The 'steak meal' they ate was definitely no perk. An assistant stage manager prepared it before the show, garnishing the chocolate mousse 'steak' with lettuce and tomatoes, and I disposed of it afterwards. On matinée afternoons, when the meal was fairly fresh, I might eat a few spoonfuls of mousse but on all other occasions I wrapped the remains in newspaper and dumped them in a dustbin. This was because I usually didn't sort out the set and props until the morning following the performance, by which time not even I could be tempted by mousse which had unappetizingly melted around lettuce and tomato garnish.

In another restaurant scene, though, there was a perk which Dad and I ensured was ours. This was a gâteau, from which only one slice was removed. I sometimes went to collect this gâteau from Fuller's, at the far end of Carnaby Street, so I could vouch for its freshness. Almost every night we'd take home a cake overflowing with chocolate flakes, cream, calories and cholesterol, and almost every night we left the cake untouched on the dining-table. At midnight, having eaten fish and chips from Burrows or something cooked by Mum, Dad and I never much fancied chocolate gâteau.

In the Swinging Sixties nudity and four-letter words began to appear on the West End stage. The producers of *Instant Marriage* played their part in promoting the new permissiveness by including a scene which featured the number 'Flipping Stripping'. None of the actresses in the cast, however, were prepared to flipping strip in public so a real stripper was recruited, presumably from one of the many strip joints in nearby Soho. While the actress-strippers paraded on stage in their underwear, the real stripper stripped down to three tiny strategically-placed red roses. For this reason we called her Rosie.

Rosie was unlike any woman I'd ever encountered. She swore like a market porter, wasn't afraid to argue with my dad and walked about naked offstage. In 1964, a couple of years before the first page three girls, a daily ogle of an unclothed adult female was not a common occurrence. It wasn't for this sixteen-year-old, at least. Rosie must have felt overdressed in her roses because as soon as she came offstage she discarded them, and then wandered around wearing only a smile while I tried to concentrate on the next scene change. Although Rosie's body was well past its 'best before' date, at first I found it extremely difficult to concentrate but after a few performances even I ignored Rosie's nakedness.

When *Instant Marriage* closed, Rosie returned to stripping in Soho's clubs. Dad and I were walking down Old Compton Street one afternoon when a familiar voice shouted "Allo, 'Arry. 'Ow you doing?" Rosie's head craned from the window of a passing taxi. 'Can't stop, 'Arry. On my way to Dean Street.' She was off to discard her roses somewhere, but onstage this time.

Some months later Dad recounted how he'd been in a West End pub, sitting on a bar stool, enjoying a glass of beer and chatting to the publican when Rosie's distinctive voice cut through the lunchtime buzz.

"'Arry Pegg. Turn round 'Arry an' let me see yer luvly face.'

Dad turned to see Rosie, mini-skirted and skimpy-topped, laughing in the doorway on platform-soled pink suede thigh boots. Before he had time to empty his glass and greet her, she hitched up her mini-skirt and ran towards him. Every head turned as Rosie tottered on her platform soles and joggled beneath her skimpy top, leapt astride the vacant bar stool next to Dad and kissed him. Before he had time to ask her what she'd like to drink, she'd ordered him another pint and herself a gin and orange, and immediately launched into an account of her most recent exploits.

According to Dad, Rosie had been talking for some minutes when she suddenly interrupted herself with the words 'Cor, fuck me, 'Arry. Me knickers.' Rosie had been so pleased to see my dad that she had completely forgotten that she was between shows and between costumes. She'd also forgotten she was temporarily knickerless. Almost anyone else would have gone scarlet with embarrassment, but not Rosie. She just laughed loudly and turned round to see what sort of audience reaction she'd got. Every head that had earlier turned to watch Rosie's bouncing front was now staring at her statuesque rear.

'Fink they'd never seen an arse before, eh, 'Arry? 'Ow's the lad?'

Christmas 1987

It's Christmas Eve, quiet
save for the stretch of Sellotape
and the careful folding of
sheeted trees and snowmen.
My first girl helps Santa
place parcels neatly near the tree,
shares his glass of Chardonnay.
My other girl doesn't stir, sure
she hears something on the roof
and sees the same
as every little boy next door.

Luke 2 ii

And it came to pass one December day
That there went out a newsletter from each school
That all should be entertained.
And this entertaining was to be made
When each head teacher decreed.
And all went forth to be entertained,
Every one to his allotted catchment area.
And Joseph went up on the stage blocks,
Out of the Reception class into the crowded hall,
To be oohed and aahed with Mary,
His arranged wife, both chosen
As being good at standing still for a long time.
And so it was that while the choir sang carols
She brought forth her teacher's daughter's doll
And wrapped him in a Mothercare blanket,
And laid him in a travel cot
Because the caretaker had hidden the school manger,
There being no room for it in the PE store.

Eleanor's Christmas Poem 1989

CHRISTMAS WRAPPING

Christmas wrapping,   Christmas Day,
What's the meaning,   what do you say?
Christmas wrapping,   Christmas Day,
Christmas crackers,   Christmas play.
Christmas presents,   Christmas pud,
Come back baby,   I wish you would.

Christmas wrapping,   Christmas Day,
Christmas story   going my way.
Christmas wrapping,   Christmas Day,
Christmas crackers,   Christmas play.
Christmas presents,   Christmas pud,
Come back baby,   I wish you would.

Jojo was a joiner,   made great chairs,
Maree, the lodger,   lived downstairs.
Jojo loved her   but Jojo was shy,
Jojo was so slow   to show Maree why
She should marry him,   relocate upstairs;
He just carried on,   made real great chairs.

One night Jojo,   asleep in bed,
Heard The Man   inside his head,
Go go Jojo,   get on down,
Dance that Maree   all round town.
Go go Jojo,   won't you try?
Go go Jojo,   don't be shy.

Downstairs Maree,   sorting socks,
Saw a vision   on her box,
A blinding light,   a flash on the screen,
A face in the night   to fashion a dream.

Jojo and Maree,   dance around town,
So so happy   in suit and gown.

Maree married him, moved upstairs,
Jojo made her a pair of chairs.

Christmas wrapping, Christmas Day,
What's the meaning, what do you say?
Christmas wrapping, Christmas Day,
Christmas crackers, Christmas play.
Christmas presents, Christmas pud,
Come back baby, I wish you would.

Jojo and Maree travelling light,
Jojo and Maree, through the night.
Jojo in his Metro, Maree in the back,
Off to Little Town to pay big tax.

Jojo and Maree travelling light,
Jojo and Maree, through the night.
Jojo driving, Maree with a map,
Lost in Palestine, off to pay tax.

Maree Maree, baby inside,
She don't want no motor ride.
Maree Maree, baby due,
Lost and tired, got no clue
Where they're going, where they've been,
Moans at Romans' poll tax scheme.

Jojo Jojo, worries growing,
Oh no oh no, started snowing.
Hello Jojo, red light blinking.
Low low petrol, Jojo's thinking.
Where oh where can this track lead?
Why oh why can't Maree map read?

Christmas wrapping, Christmas Day,
Christmas story going my way.
Christmas wrapping, Christmas Day,
Christmas crackers, Christmas play.
Christmas presents, Christmas pud,
Come back baby, I wish you would.

No rooms Jojo,   what'll you do?
No rooms Jojo,   don't be blue.
Don't wail Jojo,   go try that pub.
Real ale Jojo,   no lager club.

Maree Maree,   we'll ask in there,
Maree Maree,   someone cares.
Wrap up Maree,   don't get cold,
Stay cool Maree,   go for gold.

Lady lady   receptionist,
Maybe if you   check your list,
Any room, single room,   double will do.
We won't worry about   en suite loo.

Lady lady   receptionist,
Maybe if you   check your list,
Any room, store room,   cupboard will do.
Please don't worry   about the view.

Only a boiler room?   That will be fine.
Just the place for   that girl of mine.
A big king's castle   couldn't be better.
My lady's waiting,   I'll just go get her.

Although Jojo   has driven far,
He still helps Maree   unload the car.
Jojo and Maree   soon find their room.
A single lightbulb   lights the gloom.
Weary Jojo   quickly makes
Tea and toast,   and chocolate cake.

Maree sheds her   outdoor shoes,
Lays her head on   yesterday's news.
Both sit down for   well-earned rest,
Maree on a *Mirror*,   Jojo on *Express*.

Jojo listens to   Maree's bump,
Maree feels the   baby jump.
Jojo says it   jumps for joy,

202

Wonders is it   girl or boy?
Maree knows it   won't be long,
Sings her Jojo's   favourite song.

Christmas wrapping,   Christmas Day,
What's the meaning,   what do you say?
Christmas wrapping,   Christmas Day,
Christmas crackers,   Christmas play.
Christmas presents,   Christmas pud,
Come back baby,   I wish you would.

Christmas wrapping,   Christmas Day,
Christmas story   going my way.
Christmas wrapping,   Christmas Day,
Christmas crackers,   Christmas play.
Christmas presents,   Christmas pud,
Come back baby,   I wish you would.

Jojo wakes   to a big surprise,
Maree's baby   has just arrived.
It's a boy,   hip hop hooray,
Goes by the name   of Baby Jay.

Some will call him   'Son of God',
Not son of Jojo,   almighty odd,
'Prince of Peace'   and 'King of Kings'.
Jojo and Maree   think that swings,
Smile at the infant,   together they say,
'He'll always be   our Baby Jay.'

While Maree dresses   him in blest cotton socks,
Jojo creates a crib   from a cardboard box.
Maree kisses   her baby's nose,
Jojo counts his   fingers and toes.
Maree kisses   her baby's ears,
Jojo shares all   Maree's fears.

Hush little Maree,   don't you cry,
Jojo hears voices   in the sky.
Hush little Maree,   don't you weep,

203

Jojo's sure he just heard sheep.
Jojo hears singing, girls and boys,
Church bells ringing, Lord, what noise!

Hark the Herald, angels say,
Welcome, welcome Baby Jay.
The world outside has seen a sign
Above the 'pub grub and fine wine'.

Twinkling twinkling, a brand new star
Shows where Jojo and Maree are,
With Baby Jay, that special kid,
Sleeping in his cardboard crib.

Star of wonder, a star so bright,
Guides the good to this child of light.
From west and north from south and east,
Come women, children, man and beast.

A shepherd enters, carrying a lamb,
His flock outside in a traffic jam.
Wise men arrive in a white Rolls-Royce,
Each bearing gifts of unusual choice.

One brings exclusive designer clothes,
Benetton nappies and babygrows;
The next some sore bum zinc and myrrh cream;
The last presents a drum machine.

The cattle start lowing, Baby Jay wakes,
Gets his drums going, two minutes it takes.
Now Maree, Jojo and Sweet Baby Jay,
Can Christmas rap the night away.

Christmas wrapping, Christmas Day,
What's the meaning, what do you say?
Christmas wrapping, Christmas Day,
Christmas crackers, Christmas play.
Christmas presents, Christmas pud,
Come back baby, I wish you would.

204

Christmas wrapping,
Christmas story
Christmas wrapping,
Christmas crackers,
Christmas presents,
Come back baby,

Christmas Day,
going my way.
Christmas Day,
Christmas play.
Christmas pud,
I wish you would.

SHOES

If I'd been born in 1848 instead of 1948 I would probably write of playing barefoot in the park; reminisce about the echo of clogs up and down cobbled streets; boast that shoes had to be worn on a rota basis and pawned every Monday morning in order for our consumptive mother to buy bread. The 1950s in Ruislip Gardens, however, were easier times. Rationing had ended by then; prefabs and council estates fit for heroes had been built; children were given cheap orange juice bought from the local health clinic; everyone received medicine free on prescription when they were ill. By the middle fifties a few people had a motor car; some families owned or rented a television; an increasing number of housewives threw away their mangles and boilers and spent Mondays – the traditional washing day – with their twin tubs. Elvis Presley and the Everly Brothers were ousting Perry Como and the Andrews Sisters from the pop charts; the music of Bill Haley and his Comets caused riots in cinemas and prompted anguished discussions on *Any Questions*. Fashionable ladies wore stiletto heels, and rebellious young men wore brothel-creepers or winklepickers. I wore sensible shoes.

Although my dad had a fairly well-paid job and could get plenty of overtime to boost his earnings, he never liked spending money on expensive shoes for either himself or his children, although I suspect that he may have treated Mum to an occasional extravagant pair of dancing shoes suitable for tripping the light Masonic at a Ladies' Night at the Dorchester.

I can now understand why he didn't want our rapidly-growing feet shod expensively, but from the time I was seven until I began to pay for my own shoes I regarded my father as a miser, the man who insisted that my feet grew inside nothing more expensive than 29/11d (£1.50). It was the same for Julie and Mike, and our enforced visits to Freeman Hardy and Willis were a constant source of family friction. Dad always managed to avoid those shoe-shop conflicts, either by going to work or staying in bed, but not before he'd reminded Mum about the 29/11d ceiling and warned us kids to behave ourselves. Expecting us to behave ourselves on a shoe-buying expedition was just about as futile as occupying the Suez Canal.

Every so often Mum and her reluctant trio would troop off in the direction of the Ruislip battlefields, almost always to the aforementioned Freeman Hardy and Willis but sometimes to Bata or, worse still, to Curtess Shoes in Ruislip Manor. Thank goodness none of my friends ever caught me coming out of Curtess or carrying one of their brown paper bags. Street Cred hadn't been invented then but whatever was its 1960 equivalent would have deserted me for ever and a fortnight if I'd been sighted by someone who knew me.

As I grew older, bigger, moodier, more assertive, I managed to persuade my parents to make a few concessions in the direction of fashion shoes. My most memorable success was the purchase of a pair of black 'semi-points'. I'd asked for a pair of 'points', like those worn by my best friend Brian Bardrick, but had neither expected nor really wanted them. I was just being devious and setting up a situation where compromise would get me exactly what I wished. Wearing those semi-points on my semi-bunioned feet was painful enough, so I hate to think what winklepickers would have felt like if my plan had misfired.

In 1962 I had a weekend job in the Home & Colonial in Ruislip High Street, and was allowed a greater say in the choice of my footwear because I paid for anything over 29/11d. Later, when I worked at the Piccadilly Theatre with my dad at weekends and during school holidays, I bought all my shoes. It was at that time that I first accompanied Dad to the Soho shoe shop he patronized. Kramer's was next door to the best-known and most expensive strip club in the West End, Raymond's Revuebar, so I approached shopping trips there more enthusiastically than I ever had the much-maligned Freeman Hardy and Willis.

I was fifteen when I first saw all those publicity photo-graphs outside the club – full colour displays of dancing ladies naked save for skimpy sequined G-strings and gold stars stuck over their nipples. Being fifteen, I was at that awkward and easily embarrassed age when I didn't want my own father to catch me staring at breasts, so I just glanced nonchalantly in their direction, not lingering for fear of being classed 'a dirty young man'. However, I did devise an ingenious strategy which enabled me to get a longer second glimpse of Mr Raymond's naked lovelies.

Whenever I went with my dad to buy shoes from his friend Jack Kramer, I would deliberately select a pair that were not quite the right size. Then when we were back at the theatre I would try them on once more, 'Just to be sure they fit, Dad'. Feigning surprise because they weren't the correct size, I then returned alone to Kramer's and exchanged them. On my way in and on my way out, I stopped to ogle the strippers and speculate on how they earned their gold stars – dance technique, gymnastics, good behaviour?

Kramer's shoes were later to be much admired by most of my sixth form schoolfriends, especially when I managed to slip into our conversations the location of the shop. All the streetwise Mods, those who would have been unimpressed by my pretension, had left school after 'O' levels, but the studious ones remaining – even those with a Vespa or an ancient Ford Prefect, even those with Chelsea boots bought in Harrow or Cuban heels borrowed from an elder brother – all were envious of the exclusive Italian shoes on my size 44s. (That was further evidence of my status. 44. I could speak Continental sizing like a Continental. None of your usual Uxbridge High Street sizes 9 or 10 for *moi*.)

Dad liked shopping at Kramer's because he always got discount. I don't know where or when he first met Jack Kramer, probably in a pub in Brewer Street, but he regularly gave him complimentary tickets for shows that were not doing good business. In return for these comps, Jack gave Dad and me discount on shoes that, just like the shows, were not going to last long. At one time in the mid-sixties there was a string of shows at the Piccadilly Theatre which ran for only a few weeks. Kramer's shoes were almost as short-lived.

Life is a journey filled with ups and clichés. The suitability of the shoes on your feet can help or hinder your progress across deserts, over ice, up mountains, along dusty roads to Damascus or Dollis Hill. If you choose the right shoes, I once read in *Nova*, it can help you impress other people and make you stand out in a crowd. Why then, I'd love to know, when I was always the best-looking, best-dressed and, by far, best-shod candidate at a number of interviews for teaching jobs, did the man with brown shoes, tartan socks and blue suit last worn at his wedding ten years earlier always get the job? I admit that I told one head teacher that his questions were facile, but was that any reason for appointing blue mohair with brown brogues?

On another occasion neither the quality of my shoes nor the style of my suit helped me at all. I was interviewed for a job at a local school, a job I hadn't particularly wanted but had been persuaded to apply for by the head of the school. I think it's fair to say that I was a short-priced favourite for the post, in charge of Boys' PE and School Camp, although my odds lengthened once the interview began. It was then that the chairman of school governors, the local vicar, asked me a question prefaced with a remark which says much about the suitability of some of the people who are supposed to be managing the nation's schools.

'I don't know much about what goes on in school, but I imagine it can be exhausting, even frustrating at times,' he began. 'When you've had one of those days, how do you unwind at home?'

I felt sure that the other candidates had already told of their life-long hobby of collecting stamps, their recent introduction to the pleasures of macramé and their devotion to organizing Sunday School outings, so I thought the school governors deserved a little light relief from the monotony of the stock interview response.

'I rarely experience such days,' I lied, 'but if I do, I go home and take it out on the wife.'

Everyone except the reverend chairman laughed at my answer. He shuffled the pile of CVs in front of him, waited for the other school governors to realize that he was not amused, coughed indignantly and proceeded.

'What is your view on hamsters in the classroom?'

'Better than my wife,' I offered.

My interview soon ended and they gave the job to a music teacher who walked with a lisp and smiled at the vicar.

A local authority advisor consoled the rejected candidates by telling us how well we had all done.

'It really was very close. In the end they decided they wanted someone else who could take hymn practices. Oh yes, and they were very keen on establishing hamster breeding in the school.'

What a cageload of droppings. I knew that the successful candidate had got the job because his desert boots, navy blue wedding suit and pink shirt best fitted him for the organization of School Camp. Five years later he became a deputy head in Kent, and no doubt he will soon be one of Her Majesty's school inspectors, his pink shirt replaced by a lilac one and his desert boots swapped for brown brogues.

It's easy to see that shoe deprivation during my formative years cost me dear in later life. However, without my earlier experiences I doubt whether I would have later had the incentive to get myself into the real heartland of Swinging London, the King's Road in Chelsea and Carnaby Street. The journey to these places, which had begun with the long trudge to Freeman Hardy and Willis in Ruislip High Street and continued with the canter to Kramer's, was completed after high altitude training at the Marble Arch end of Oxford Street. In the summer of 1965 I was passing the Shoe Rack, a shop which sold slightly sub-standard and end-of-range oddment shoes. Sellotaped to the window near the shop door was a card which said 'PART-TIME STAFF WANTED APPLY WITHIN' – so I went within and applied.

At the till near the door I spoke to a small, smartly-suited man aged about twenty-five and told him that I was very interested in a part-time job. He informed me that he was only the assistant manager, asked someone else to take over on the till, and showed me to the rear of the shop where he introduced me to the manager, a tall, moustached, more than slightly overweight man in his fifties called Sargeant. I remember that he wore spectacles with strong lenses, a chalk-striped navy blue suit and expensive-looking black patent casual shoes. He also smoked virtually nonstop. At that stage of my life my near-paranoid abhorrence of cigarette smokers had yet to develop fully so I politely answered his few brief questions about my previous shop experience and current status. I told him about my Saturday jobs in supermarkets, my occasional backstage work in the theatre and, I fibbed, helping out at Kramer's once or twice. Mr Sargeant was

211

suitably impressed, or – much more likely – seriously under-staffed, and a job was mine.

Initially I worked full-time at the Shoe Rack during my summer holiday in 1965. Thereafter I worked every Friday evening and Saturday, plus the occasional extra day at busier times such as before and after Christmas. When I'd been at the shop a few months I spoke nicely to Mr Sargeant and got Julie a Saturday job. At that time she was an apprentice dressmaker in a couturier's sweatshop near Bond Street, earning a pittance for long hours of demanding work, so she was very pleased to have some regular extra income.

Travelling to work with Julie on Saturday mornings caused a minor problem since I would never sit with her in a Smoking carriage. In those days half the train was allocated to people like Julie, people who insisted on their right to make themselves ill while littering the floor of the world with used matches and cigarette ends.

Our Saturday mornings on the Central Line always ran the same way. On the platform at Ruislip Gardens, as we waited for the train, I stood and read my *Guardian* while Julie went inside the smoke-filled waiting room for a quick drag; we then sat together in a Non-Smoking carriage for about half a dozen stops; at this point Julie transferred to a Smoking carriage for a further nicotine fix before rejoining me at Bayswater Road for the final leg of our journey to Marble Arch. Anyone sitting nearby would have been intrigued by the constant disappearances and regular reappearances of the mini-skirted blonde with the Mary Quant hairstyle, but the family resemblance was so marked that we wouldn't, at least, have been mistaken for tiffing lovers.

There was one particular Saturday morning when our fellow passengers would have been nauseated rather than intrigued by my sister's strange activity. It was late December, and Julie had been to a pre-Christmas celebration on the Friday night, during which she had mixed rather too many alcoholic drinks with a large quantity of Twiglets and an unspecified number of assorted vol-au-vents. Waking Julie on any Saturday morning was only marginally safer than singing 'The Red Flag' beneath Norman Tebbit's bedroom window, but waking Julie on that particular morning was more dangerous than placing your head in that same Tebbit's mouth and attempting to play an accompaniment to 'The Red Flag' on his teeth. I coaxed Julie's head off her pillow with a mug of sweet black coffee, and five minutes later she had locked herself in the bathroom for the usual lengthy make-up session.

I might have guessed that things were not as they ought to have been when Julie emerged, after three bangs on the bathroom door, minus her Dusty Springfield double-length false eyelashes. I doubt if even her most recent boyfriend would have recognized Julie without those eyelashes. Julie, who dressed fashionably and had always been an attractive girl, had more than her fair share of boyfriends. She had an engaging personality, as illustrated by the size of the quarterly phone bills; she had a reasonable figure, as illustrated by holiday snaps of her at Butlins circa 1966 in a parade of 'Miss Lovely Legs' contestants; she also had striking blonde hair cut à la mode de Twiggy and her friend Carol Pugh – Julie's friend, that is, and not, as far as I know, Twiggy's. Julie will admit, though, that her complexion was far from perfect, being sometimes pink and blotchy and at other times blotchy and pink. I think that the sheer volume and weight of her mascara, perfume, powder, eyeliner and synthetic eyelashes were significant factors contributing to Julie's problem skin but she will doubtless argue that she used all that make-up as camouflage. On this particular Saturday morning no amount of make-up could ever have camouflaged Julie's ashen features, though. A Balaclava helmet would have been the only practical solution.

As we went slowly down Stafford Road towards Ruislip Gardens Station Julie's face became greyer, her walking more laboured, her speech much more pained and reluctant. I doubted if she would manage the ascent from ticket office to platform, but with the aid of a friendly London Transport employee we inched our way to the summit of the stairs and staggered into an opportunely-arrived train. Fortunately for me, the carriage was a Non-Smoker but Julie thought she needed a cigarette and shuffled pathetically to an adjoining carriage when we reached the next station, South Ruislip. I warned her against this, declaring that thirty minutes with her head out of the window would be more beneficial than three fags. But Pegg by name, pig-headed by nature, we're all the same, and Julie was determined to follow her nose into the Smoking carriage rather than listen to her elder brother's wise counsel.

Two stops down the line at Greenford, appropriately enough, Julie appeared green-faced in my carriage.

'Hello,' I remarked to myself, 'Julie's not well.'

Julie confirmed this. 'I'm not well,' she moaned, just prior to a perfectly executed demonstration of projectile vomiting onto both Greenford's concrete platform and the wooden floor of my carriage near the guard's door. Fortunately, no guard was there. Fortunately, too, there were only a few other passengers sharing my carriage, all sitting at the far end, all staring into their daily paper and none of them daring to believe what they could hear Julie doing. In the rear carriage a fortunate Jamaican guard named Gladstone, blissfully unaware of the drama unfolding half a train ahead of him, pressed a button and the doors of the train closed, the door nearest my sister neatly bisecting the evidence of the previous night's over-indulgence. The train moved off in slow motion, leaving a part of Greenford forever Julie and part of Julie's party forever Greenford. At Perivale our carriage was evacuated, speedily but without panic.

Julie and I found our way to the nearest platform seat to wait for the next train and to allow Julie time enough to fill her lungs with cold December air. The newspaper readers from the far end fled in the opposite direction. No doubt they lowered their papers to stare at us over their headlines as the train moved away, but we never saw them. I had my back to the train and was examining the rear of the Hoover factory. Julie had her back to the wind and was lighting up another cigarette.

The assistant manager at the Shoe Rack was from the Seychelles or Mauritius, or some other island, but an island more exotic than Sheppey or Wight and one where the natives spoke French. Louis was his name but Mr Sargeant called him Lewis. The two of them managed the staff in very contrasting ways, Louis being quietly-spoken, considerate and sympathetic, whereas the Sargeant Major, as we nicknamed the manager, was loud, rude, arrogant and intimidating. Needless to say, Louis was well-liked while Mr Sargeant was much-loathed.

Initially I got on well with Mr Sargeant and quite liked him, but that changed after an incident in January 1966. One of my reasons for quite liking the manager was the errands I ran for him, often to another shop to collect stock but mostly to Selfridges' Food Hall to buy him something for lunch. My visits to other shops gave me an opportunity to see a much more glamorous side of selling shoes as I frequented the stockrooms of Mondaine and Pinet. If I had a stack of shoe boxes to bring back I hailed a black cab and travelled in unaccustomed style, observing the hustle and bustle of West End shopping from the leather comfort of my very own taxi.

Chauffeured excursions were rare treats, but my walks across Oxford Street to Selfridges were regular occurrences, Mr Sargeant sending me there for an item of exotica totally alien to my suburban culinary experience, namely eggplant. When he first asked me to buy some for his lunch I thought he was playing a joke, and even when Louis confirmed that just such a fruit grew profusely on his island home I remained unconvinced. In Selfridges it was sold ready-prepared and packed in a plastic container to take away. Mr Sargeant devoured the entire contents while looking through the security mirror in his office, his eyes scanning the interior of the shop for evidence of shoplifting or, worse still, signs that his staff might be enjoying themselves.

At the same time as I discovered the existence of eggplant in the Food Hall at Selfridges I stumbled upon a treasure house of epicurean delights unheard of in Ruislip's Home & Colonial, let alone Frank Norman or Pearks in Ruislip Gardens. Not a sniff of the nose from the eggplant counter were:

> salami garlands, garlic, green peppers,
> peppers yellow and red, bread with poppy seeds,
> pizzas, pies, quiches, tarts with peaches,
> tarts with black cherries, blackberry and quince jam,
> Parma ham, Parmesan, cheese from France,
> free range quails' eggs, snails and frogs' legs,
> tea from China, wine from Chile,
> sauce from Soya, beans dwarf, beans French,
> mustard from Dijon, mussels from the Mediterranean,
> terrines and pâtés, baklava, laver bread,
> red mullet, ready-cooked chicken breasts,
> pesto, pasta, filo pastry and filled sandwiches.

I sometimes bought myself sandwiches for lunch, and very occasionally I would purchase a small portion of Melton Mowbray pie, but I could only feast my imagination at most of the counters, my gastronomic ambition painfully restricted by the breadline payment which rattled inside the brown envelope given me each Saturday by Mr Sargeant.

One crisp but sunny Saturday morning in January 1966 the manager asked me to walk over to the post office in

216

Wigmore Street to buy stamps, some for postage plus the week's National Insurance stamps. I had done this on a number of previous occasions, so confidently took the shopping list and money, six five-pound notes, put them in my trouser pocket and proudly donned my new brown mid-length Aquascutum raincoat which I'd just bought in the January sales. When Mr Sargeant made a most uncharacteristic complimentary remark about it, I duly gave a twirl and modelled some of its finer features: fashionable Prussian collar; expensive-looking lining; fly-front buttoning; special slits just inside the pockets that gave the wearer quick and easy access to his trousers and jacket (a dubious feature, I always thought, being there for the benefit only of dirty old members of the dirty old raincoat brigade). . .

'OK, that'll do,' interrupted Mr Sargeant, gently pushing me into the shop. 'They close at twelve.'

It was about ten-thirty and it would only take me about ten minutes to walk to the post office so I sneaked into the Claude Gill bookshop next door for a browse. If I got back late to the Shoe Rack I would tell old Sargeant that there had been a very long queue in the post office.

In the Wigmore Street post office I joined the end of a very long queue. In front of me was a typically cosmopolitan file of post office users, all of them patiently waiting for service from the sole counter assistant who was not closed: an old lady who wanted two airmail letters, one for her youngest son in Australia and the other for her only surviving sister in Boston; a taxi driver after Premium Bonds for his latest granddaughter, newly arrived at Hammersmith Hospital just last night at seven o'clock; two German tourists with postcards of Coldstream Guards marching down the Mall and needing stamps for Paraguay; a tobacconist with bags of florins and half-crowns ready for banking; the Cypriot manager of the nearby Rio Sandwich Bar with a brown paper parcel for posting to cousins in Nicosia; a little girl waiting to buy her weekly savings stamp, standing with her dad who looks worried because his wife has been ill and the television licence should have been renewed months ago; a cheery Barbadian bus conductress dreaming of cruising home and the gifts she'd buy her family if she won the football pools with the three-bob postal order she was about to buy.

After I had speculated about my fellow queuers, I posed in my raincoat and casually demonstrated some of its unique Aquascutum hallmarks. Each time I shuffled nearer the counter I checked that the post office wall clock was five minutes faster than my watch until, nine shuffles and nine timechecks later, it was my turn to be served.

By the time I had handed over my list and the counter assistant had scrutinized it, twice,

and by the time he had carefully counted out all of the stamps, again twice,

and by the time he had checked his adding up, twice,

and given me my change, twice because he got it wrong by a threepenny bit first time,

and by the time I emerged into the sunlight and traffic noise of Wigmore Street it was twenty past eleven. I had been out of the shop for almost an hour. Nevertheless, I still intended calling in at Selfridges for my mid-morning snack so I pocketed the stamps and change and hurried towards the Food Hall. Elated by the admiring glances that I felt my new raincoat was getting, I selected and paid for an exotically-filled sandwich which I stylishly demolished as I strolled back to the Shoe Rack.

Outside Mothercare I wiped the last evidence from the corners of my mouth and dropped the empty sandwich bag into a litter bin. Inside the Shoe Rack Mr Sargeant was standing behind Louis, peering over his shoulder at ten-shilling notes, pound notes and fivers trapped inside the till. He looked at his wrist watch with an exaggerated gesture of his right arm, from which I inferred he was not too pleased with me.

'Sorry I'm late,' I chirped before he said anything, 'but you know what the queues are like on a Saturday.'

He followed me to the back of the shop and into the staff room where I felt inside my raincoat pocket for the insurance stamps. They weren't there. I tried the other pocket, the left one, but they weren't there either. Mr Sargeant began to look really cross. As I checked my trouser pockets for the stamps that I'd bought not twenty minutes earlier I began to panic. No sign of them anywhere.

'I don't understand,' I whined. 'They were here just now.'

I whipped my raincoat off to see if the stamps could have found their way into the space between coat and lining.

'Here's the change, three and nine,' I announced, putting four coins on the table in the staff room.

'Sod the change! Where are all those stamps?' demanded Mr Sargeant, his usual arrogance giving way to menace.

Two women assistants, who had been gossiping over coffee just moments earlier, drained their cups, cut short their break and scuttled out of the staff room into the shop. As I described my movements between ten-thirty and eleven-thirty, the visit to the Food Hall slipped out, thereby compounding my loss of the stamps.

'Well you'd better get back there and find them,' Mr Sargeant proclaimed, pointing his right arm in the general direction of Selfridges. I picked up my raincoat and hurried through the crowded shop, customers staring at me as I brushed aside Julie's 'What's up?' to begin retracing my journey to and from the post office.

I scanned roads and pavements and Food Hall floors with minesweeper precision; I asked a Selfridges' pieman, a patrolling policeman and the post office checker, twice, but I was out of luck. The stamps had disappeared forever, found and kept by person or persons unknown after I had inadvertently posted them through the dubious feature in my new raincoat.

I was out of pocket, too. I had to pay for those stamps, a pound a week deducted from my wage packet at source by the Sargeant Major. He still sent me for eggplant so I continued my exploration of Selfridges' Food Hall. Louis went for the stamps, though.

The workers at the Shoe Rack were a mixed bunch unified by a common need for extra income. There were a couple of young people who, like Julie and me, worked only one or two days each week. I got on particularly well with Ramona, a West Indian girl with unruly hair which she wanted to be Afro-ed in the style of Marsha Hunt. I remember travelling on an Underground train with her once, and feeling very liberal and daring as dozens of morose white office workers and shoppers gazed at us intolerantly while Ramona told me about her family in Holloway and church-going on Sundays. If I'd stayed at the Shoe Rack I might have fulfilled one of my lifetime ambitions and gone with Ramona to a black revivalist church, banged a tambourine and shouted 'Praise the Lord!' during the sermon.

I remember only three of the Shoe Rack regulars, Leila, who came from an unknown Arab country, and two East European Jewish sisters called Fay and Hilda. The sisters did not get on well with Leila but not, as you might guess, because of religious or historical differences. The plain truth is that nobody got on well with Leila. I suspect that even Leila's shadow did not get on well with Leila. I suspect, too, that Leila's Arab place of origin was Libya and that she was a founder member of Colonel Ghadaffi's urban terrorist guerrillas.

Leila's appearance belied the peace-shattering effect that she had at our end of Oxford Street. She was a frail and tiny grey-haired woman who always wore old unco-ordinated cast-off clothes beneath her blue uniform, laddered stockings on her bruised and varicose-veined legs, scuffed and ancient pointed shoes upon her ever-active feet. She prowled the aisles of the Shoe Rack, a bird of prey disguised as a scarecrow, ready to rob the other assistants of sales or claim an innocent customer as her own. 'Just looking' meant nothing to Leila as she glided on the fetid trade winds inside the Shoe Rack, her mission commission. Only the strongest-willed customers ever fled from Leila's talons without an unwanted pair of platform-soled slingbacks or canvas casuals.

The two sisters, especially Hilda, were no match for Leila, either. Hilda, in fact, was one of the most vulnerable adults I have ever met, and used to wander around the shop muttering to herself like a madwoman. She and Fay were aged about forty, but looked at least sixty with their severely cut silver hair, sunken eyes and hollowed cheeks. I later learned that the sisters had been incarcerated by the Nazis during the war, and it was rumoured that they had seen their parents marched into the gas chambers. The part-timers tried to help Fay and Hilda by assigning our sales to them. We were paid per session, and not by commission, so we could afford to be generous. Even Mr Sargeant took pity on the sisters, turning a blind eye to our commission conspiracy and only employing Hilda as a favour to Fay, who would otherwise have been forced to give up her job and look after her severely disturbed sister at home. Julie once visited them in their flat near Marble Arch, a damp, cramped and cluttered couple of rented rooms that Julie thought 'a slum'. It must have been a palace for Fay and Hilda after the wartime conditions they'd endured.

People of my age hadn't directly experienced any of the horrors of war. I remember seeing plenty of bomb sites in London; I knew that an uncle had died on service in the Far East; I'd been inside an air raid shelter in the grounds of my primary school; and all children in the fifties discussed what their parents had 'been in the war'. Nothing I knew or talked about, though, and nothing I ever saw on television or in the cinema told me about the horror of war as much as the story and sight of those sisters.

By helping Fay and Hilda we incurred the wrath of Leila, of course. I never minded this and, indeed, enjoyed antagonizing her as often as was possible. The easiest method was to 'give' her difficult customers, ones I had identified as time-wasters or browsers. Leila never understood the 'just looking' attitude of the British shopper, being more used to the adversarial customer-trader relations of the souk. If Mr Sargeant had allowed her, Leila would have happily introduced barter and price-haggling into Oxford Street, I'm sure.

We all tried to sabotage Leila's commercial activities but her appetite for work was insatiable; we tried to encourage the sisters but their hearts and thoughts were somewhere else; we also tried to persuade our customers to buy shoes they didn't really want, but none of us possessed Leila's killer instinct.

Eventually, though, I developed an ingenious technique to persuade even the most reluctant customers to buy from me. I first learned this technique one afternoon when I was assisting a customer to buy a pair of shoes she really neither needed nor wanted. She claimed that the shoes I was attempting to sell her were too small, a Continental size 35. And anyway, she insisted, she would much prefer a black pair with buttons, like those bought by her sister the day before. She ignored my declaration that the navy blue ones with a buckle could still be seen in the Bond Street window of Mondaine for £20, and insisted I look for a black pair in the stock room.

Mr Sargeant found a black pair with buttons, but they were also size 35.

'Watch me,' he commanded, taking them into the shop

to show my customer. 'Good afternoon, madam, I am the manager,' he introduced himself, emphasizing the 'dam' and 'I am'. He then proceeded to flatter 'madam' about her choice of the black buttoned style in preference to the navy buckled model picked by the 'junior sales assistant back there in the stockroom'. He sneered in the direction of the security mirror, behind which I stood swearing to myself as I observed his Machiavellian sales patter.

'When I was in our Mayfair branch just last Monday,' he boasted, 'covering for my friend Royston, the manager, who was on jury service, I sold two pairs of these to Princess Margaret – one in black and the other navy blue.'

Madam's expression indicated that she was hooked, enticed by the royal worm that old Sargeant was dangling in front of her.

'Unfortunately, we don't have the black pair in your size, but if you will permit me I can stretch them for you,' and all the time he was caressing the shoes to point out some of their most desirable features. 'This Brazilian leather is especially supple and once they have been stretched professionally these shoes will be so comfortable. Indeed, I am sure that madam will feel like a princess herself wearing these.'

Leaving my customer just long enough to consider the implication of the words 'professionally' and 'princess' he asked, 'Shall I stretch them for you?' adding 'And if you are not happy when you have worn them around the house for a day, bring them back and I will gladly refund your money.'

This was the final lure for madam. If she hadn't been impressed by the original Mondaine price, Princess Margaret, Mayfair and supple Brazilian leather, the offer of a refund convinced her and she consented to the stretching of court shoes and credulity.

Mr Sargeant came into the stockroom from the shop and asked me to fetch the stretching machine. I must have looked like a puzzled monkey to his grinning gorilla.

'Where is it?' I asked.

'Just there,' he declared, pointing to a broom leaning against a stack of shoe boxes, and he reached for it with the exaggerated triumphant flourish of Paul Daniels at a chimpanzees' tea party. 'You'll like this, but not a lot,' he might have said, but since this was 1965 and not 1985 he ordered me to 'Watch this' and proceeded to insert the broom handle inside the right shoe and gently massage the toe and sides between his palms and the rounded top of the handle. After a few moments he gave the left shoe the same treatment, before taking both out to my customer.

'Try these, please. Madam will notice the difference, I am confident,' he predicted, once again emphasizing 'dam' and 'I am'. Madam duly complied, tried the shoes on and agreed that they now fitted her perfectly. Yes, she would take them, thank you very much, but just to make Mr Sargeant's day she also bought the navy blue pair with the buckle. Princess Margaret, my shoe horn! I bet madam scanned newspaper photos and TV film reports for years, squealing with delight to her sister, 'There they are! She's wearing the navy ones. Don't like that hat much.'

And I imagined Princess Margaret, visiting the Fleet Air Arm Museum or opening a drug and alcohol re-habilitation unit in Windsor turning her back to a camera lens and whispering to an equerry, 'My bloody feet are agony. If I ever see that smarmy fat git in Mondaine again I'll show him what to do with his bloody stretching machine.'

While I worked at the Shoe Rack I practised and per-fected my broom-handle technique until I'm sure I would have won a Queen's Award to the Shoe Industry if I hadn't sought fame and misfortune elsewhere. Whenever I subsequently faced a customer who felt that his or her shoes were not comfortable enough I, like my mentor, would cobble together a catalogue of desirable qualities relating to the craftmanship, country of origin, original Bond Street price and my previous clients, before offering the assistance of the latest shoe-trade technology, the stretching machines. Note the plural 'machines'. After the briefest reference to stretching I would casually enquire 'Do you mind which machine I use, the gas steam stretcher or the electrically-powered one?' The customer always asked if there was any difference, and I would then detail the advantages and disadvantages of both machines.

'Well, for these shoes, which are really fine quality, I'd recommend the gas steam machine from Italy. It's much kinder to soft leather. Mind you, the German machine is easier to operate and much quicker than the steam stretcher.'

Completely baffled by my conscienceless science, the customer inevitably chose exactly what I'd recommended and I would disappear into the back of the shop with the ill-fitting shoes, collecting the broom from a corner of the stockroom on my way to the staff room.

'Another stretching job, eh, Steve?' someone would ask. 'German electric or Italian gas?'

'Zee gas, bambino, All zee way from Milano.'

'In which case, you'll have time for a coffee.'

'Si, uno cappuccino. Grazie, mate.'

After my mug of Maxwell House I would return to the shop and apologize to my customer. 'Sorry about the delay, but I did warn you that the steam machine was slower. I won't be long now, though.' And once again I'd disappear, emerging minutes later from the stockroom carrying the shoes with some difficulty and rubbing a hand. 'That blooming machine, it caught my hand again. That's twice this week,' I'd complain, inventing a little tale about the idiosyncrasies of all Italian stretching machines; how ours needed a service but was soon to be replaced by an updated Austrian machine;

how a similar machine in a shop in Nottingham had caught fire and badly burned the manager . . . Oh, the untruths I was extravagant with in my pursuit of sales. The customer, previously ignorant of the dangerous life of shoe-shop assistants, listened in amazement, regarded me with admiration and tried on the shoes.

'Yes, they do fit perfectly now,' he grudgingly admitted or she gratefully praised. 'I'll take them.'

Neither pay nor working conditions at the Shoe Rack were good but no two days were ever the same so life there was unpredictable, entertaining and often educational. For example, I had never heard of aubergines before going to Selfridges for Mr Sargeant – matzos, garlic salt and lilac toilet tissue being just about the most exotic elements of my supermarket experiences in Sudbury Town and Ruislip. Something else introduced to me at the Shoe Rack was the word 'mezzanine', a word somewhat alien to working-class culture in the mid-sixties. The mezzanine floor in the Shoe Rack was a storage area above the staff room, reached via a set of shaky aluminium steps. Mr Sargeant kept all the ladies' boots there, just so he could tell mini-skirted salesgirls like Julie, 'You'll find them on the mezzanine. I'll hold the steps for you.' Dirty old manager.

Probably the most revelatory educational experience occurred one summer afternoon when a tall, dark, leggy lady came into the shop. She wore a split skirt which was just a little longer than a mini, no stockings on strong, shapely legs and black pointed stiletto-heel shoes on size 42 feet. The top three buttons of her white silk blouse were tantalizingly undone, the silver crucifix on the chain around her neck pointing at a hint of cleavage. Her hairstyle was not unlike Leila's – coarse, dry and wild – but a wide bandanna attempted to keep it under control. Her nose and eyes were large, her cheeks pockmarked, the whole face hardly softened by the merest trace of

226

make-up. I approached her to offer assistance, but Mr Sargeant intervened and told me to take my tea break. Minutes later he summoned me to look through the two-way security mirror into the shop. 'She is a he. A transvestite,' he whispered, pointing at the front of the silk blouse as I gazed in disbelief at her size 42s, legs and split skirt. 'She likes me to serve her whenever she comes in. Very shy really. Needs someone who won't take the Michael, someone discreet, someone tolerant. She used to buy her shoes from me when I was at Bond Street.'

Well, I'd never have described Mr Sargeant as discreet or tolerant. However, he was right about the sensitive transvestite preferring his help. He/she bought an expensive pair of red, Italian, high-heeled winklepickers with an exclusive Kurt Geiger label plus two pairs of Pinet court shoes. And all without the aid of the stretching machine.

After the episode with the insurance stamps I grew disenchanted with working in the Shoe Rack. Mr Sargeant became more obnoxious in his treatment of everyone, even the sisters, so I sounded out the possibility of transferring elsewhere. One of the Saturday assistants, a lad my age called George, was the son of one of the company directors. George left the Shoe Rack to work in a Ravel shop closer to his home but I kept in touch with him, meeting him once or twice for a drink and letting him have some complimentary tickets for a show at the Piccadilly. George introduced me to his father once, in offices behind Mondaine in New Bond Street, and asked him if there were any Saturday jobs vacant. I was offered a few weeks' trial period at the King's Road branch of Ravel, which I accepted without hesitation. Mr Sargeant was not very happy, saying that he wouldn't have me back if I failed my trial. I had no thoughts of failure, though, only a head filled with dreams of Swinging London.

I worked no more than four weeks in the King's

Road, Chelsea, and I never met Mary Quant, Barbara Hulanicki, Justin de Villeneuve or Rod Stewart, although I once bumped into Helen and Arthur Loman coming out of a supermarket, complaining loudly about poor service and the price of tonic water. Helen and Arthur were friends of my father, fellow members of the Green Room Club and as far removed from Swinging London as Arthur Scargill from the House of Windsor. I never purchased anything from a trendy Chelsea boutique, frightened away by either the high prices of the goods on display in the window or the high camp of the staff on display inside. I did buy my all-time favourite pair of shoes while working in the King's Road, though, brown and buckled Clansman. I also bought Ros a tiny toy koala, from Peter Jones in Sloane Square. More importantly, I successfully passed my trial and was offered a Saturday job in Carnaby Street.

Piro Shoes had three shops there, a men's shop diagonally opposite a women's shop at the crossroads in the middle of the street, both of them very tiny, and a much larger newly-opened shop at the Golden Square end of the street where I went to sell shoes to the feet of both genders. And all nations, for Carnaby Street was already a tourist attraction and my shop had been opened to cater for the increasing number of foreign visitors who included the place in their tour itinerary. The full-time staff included several 'birds' who could help any tourists who didn't speak English. An Austrian girl, Chris, spoke German, Italian and French; her Danish flatmate, Vibeke, served Scandinavians; and two New York girls smoothed out Anglo-American linguistic difficulties. I contributed my schoolboy French (much improved following a 1966 summer holiday near Perpignan) and was even interviewed by a French radio crew who wanted me to explain, in French, the origin and significance of the word 'camp'. They asked me, I hasten to add, only because I claimed to speak French well and not because of the way I walked or the colour of my shirt. No mincing gait or pink shirts from me, sweetie.

The same could not be said for Malcolm, the manager of the shop. He was definitely a pink shirt and matching walk man, but a gentle person who was popular with everyone who worked for him. He was not unlike the camp and queenly dressers I encountered in the theatre, and the atmosphere in his shop was always light-hearted and relaxed, even if it wasn't as way out and wild as I had hoped for.

The truth is that Carnaby Street had been innovative and exciting only for a couple of years. In the past I had often used it as a short cut when walking between Oxford Circus Underground Station and the Piccadilly Theatre, and so I had seen how the original boutiques – John Stephen, John and Him – had been joined by Irvine Sellars, Take Six, Trecamp, Topper and Raoul. Later came the souvenir shops, complete with Carnaby Gonks, Swinging London mugs and Union Jack accessories. After that the street was pedestrianized, sanitized and fully commercialized for the purpose of fleecing tourists. Even by the time I worked there it was well on the way to becoming the tacky tourist trap it is today.

For most of my generation Swinging London and its accompanying permissiveness were myths created by newspapers to increase circulation figures. I was in the West End every Saturday, and every night in the summer, eighteen, blond, tall and slim; I wore black flared dancer's trousers, brown Clansman, and a tailored cowboy shirt from The Westerner in Old Compton Street; Vibeke got me free entry to Le Kilt discotheque and I frequently drank at Pop's Club with dancers from the Windmill; in the summer of 1965 Peter O'Toole bought me a drink every Thursday; Barry Humphries introduced me to the sophisticated taste of Cinzano and tonic; I worked with a man who once drove to a party in Brian Epstein's Rolls-Royce . . . My list of qualifications was impeccable,

I thought, yet whenever I went to parties I was never offered drugs or a small part in an orgy, just warm beer from a plastic cup and two cushions and a dusty rug to sleep with.

Looking back on the Swinging Sixties Scene, I don't now regret being a mere observer since swinging along with hedonistic activities often led to later injury and indignity. No furtive visits to the VD clinic or Alcoholics Anonymous for me, thank heavens, and no drug overdoses, bad trips or attempted suicides. WAIT A MOMENT! I'm sounding like a right pompous cleveritch in the unmentionables. Looking back at the Swinging Sixties Scene, I don't NOW regret being a mere observer, it's true, but at the time I was livid.

It's also true that working in the West End meant that I was never misled by the glamour implicit in so much contemporary reporting, and I got a glimpse behind enough tatty façades to know that I was not missing out on very much. Still, everyone expects to experience some tatty glamour in their youth. I never did. Whatever happened to other young men in the sixties and seventies avoided me. I'll give you two examples.

1965. I was working at the Piccadilly Theatre on *Enrico*, a big musical. This girl dresser with hair like Marianne Faithfull but the face of an angel said she could get me a lot of work as a fashion model. When I spoke to my dad about this his reaction wasn't encouraging.

'Bleedin' lot of twaddle,' was probably his considered response to my suggestion that I go along to an address in Earls Court for an audition. 'Load of bumhole bandits in that business. You get your "A" levels out of the way first, and then we'll see.'

By the time 'A' levels were out of the way, *Enrico* had closed, the dresser was touring Austria with *The Sound of Music* and I was too old to begin a career in modelling.

1970. Was that the year of the Bob Dylan concert on the Isle of Wight? And where was I? The answer, my friend, was blowing in the wind not very far away on the Isle of Purbeck, staying with Ros and my family in one wing of a 16th-century manor house near Swanage.

These two examples show why I was a mere observer. I was never in the right place at the right time, always too many miles west or a few months late. Today I don't mind admitting that I put the 'miss' in permissive, but when I was eighteen, blond, tall and slim, wearing black flared dancer's trousers, brown Clansman and a tailored cowboy shirt from The Westerner in Old Compton Street . . .

At your first infant's Christmas play
You join the faithful who have come
To school or church or village hall,
And find a chair where you might see
All that will be Bethlehem
From first carol to final call.

At your first infant's Christmas play
You recall scenes from your own infancy.
A recorder group signals start,
Your heart is on a trampoline,
Your mouth in a desert.
And all that template scenery,
Perfect hills under a blackboard sky,
One end of a barn, the roof of an inn,
Town and country met beneath a star.

At your first infant's Christmas play
You search for the star and sigh,
Wonder where the years have gone.
It seems like only dreams away
You wrapped her safe against the world,
Thanked a nurse and drove her home.
And how long will she stay an angel,
Naive as Mary, gentle as a shepherd,
Humble as Joseph, confident as a king?
How soon before her sleep is troubled,
Fingernails bitten, eyes like a sea,
Heart broken by another man's song?

I can't wake you with a kiss each morning,
trace my fingers round your face, rub your nose.
I can't carry breakfast to your bedroom,
squeeze an orange, slice bread, butter your toast.

I can't button cuffs for you or brush your hair,
find your socks and schoolbooks, hold your lunch box.
I can't skip with you down the road, hand in hand
and swinging arms, head thrown back laughing at the
     tree tops.

I can't stand and watch you in the playground,
chasing Amy, racing after Vicky's friends.
I can't cuddle you if you stumble or
be waiting at the gate when school ends.

I can't ask you what you've done,
read your news book, sing along with the latest song.
I can't take you to the park, bounce on a castle
or push you – Higher! Higher! – on a swing.

I can't surprise you on my own,
buy you hair slides, jigsaws, games.
I can't show you Shakespeare, ballet,
Punch and Judy, pantomime.

I can't say that we'll go swimming,
splash your back, build a palace by a Charmouth sea.
I can't show you ammonites or fool's gold, rock pools
where monsters wait to scare a princess on a
     summer day.

I can't live trapped with my dreams in a single room
while you and the world are out there dancing.
I can't tap my feet, waiting for you to come home
with a secret for me, whispers between friends.

I can't wake you with a kiss each morning . . .

my daddy

By: Eleanor

myself

By: Eleanor

JUST SOME CONFESSIONS
OF A STORYTELLER

For more than half of my daughter's life I have been ill, growing weaker and more disabled almost daily. I often wonder what she thinks and feels as she observes my gradual deterioration. Sometimes, too, I wonder how she'll remember me. I also worry that her only recollection might be of a thin, voiceless man sitting alone and staring into his past. That was why I started writing *Just Some Stories for Eleanor*. I hope that they tell her more about me than old photographs and other people's memories.

Eleanor is great fun, an all-dancing, all-singing, all-action contrast to me. She leads a very busy life, presently enjoying tap and ballet dancing, gymnastics, swimming and riding, in addition to school. I would dearly love to join her for all of these activities – even school! – and I have a headful of ordinary pleasures which I wish we could share. Unfortunately we can't do together those simple things that most other dads and daughters probably take for granted, so Eleanor tells me about her world while I write about mine. At the moment she is too young to be intrigued by the titles of my stories, and is much more interested in watching children's television than listening to any of them. However, Eleanor knows that the stories are written for her. A few years from now I'm sure she'll understand why.

22 November 1990

NOT WITHOUT MY DAUGHTER

BY BETTY MAHMOODY

'You are here for the rest of your life. Do you understand? You are not leaving Iran. You are here until you die.'

Betty Mahmoody and her husband, Dr Sayyed Bozorg Mahmoody ('Moody'), came to Iran from the USA to meet Moody's family. With them was their four-year-old daughter, Mahtob. Appalled by the squalor of their living conditions, horrified by what she saw of a country where women are merely chattels and Westerners are despised, Betty soon became desperate to return to the States. But Moody, and his often vicious family, had other plans. Mother and daughter became prisoners of an alien culture, hostages of an increasingly tyrannical and violent man.

Betty began to try to arrange an escape. Evading Moody's sinister spy network, she secretly met sympathizers opposed to Khomeini's savage regime. But every scheme that was suggested to her meant leaving Mahtob behind for ever . . .

Eventually, Betty was given the name of a man who would plan their perilous route out of Iran, a journey that few women or children had ever made. Their nightmare attempt to return home began in a bewildering snowstorm . . .

'The horrific situation in which Betty Mahmoody found herself would give any loving mother nightmares. Hers is an amazing story of a woman's courage and total devotion to her child that will have you rooting for them along every inch of their treacherous journey'
Susan Oudot, *Woman's Own*

'Compelling drama . . . fascinating, if disturbing . . . a moving story of one person's fortitude, courage and faith'
New York Times Book Review

0 552 13356 6

Now a major film starring Sally Field

STARLINGS LAUGHING

BY JUNE VENDALL CLARK

'In common with the very best examples of the "Africa" genre, this book is a good deal more than its spectacular sunsets, dangerous animals, diseases and droughts. June Vendall Clark's elegantly crafted autobiography ... chronicles the struggle to establish a wildlife reserve long before it became the fashion to do so. Few books can live up to the publisher's blurb; this one does'
Observer

June Vendall Clark came to love the magic and mysticism, the wildlife, people and land of Southern Africa during the forty-three years she spent there. She lived with her philandering husband, Robert Kay, first on Far Lamorna, a farm in the Rhodesian bush, then in a converted amphibious transporter on the edge of the Kalahari Desert. For eight years June and Robert organised safaris, hunted crocodiles for a living and learned the practical lessons of survival in the wild. There were endless financial problems, tropical diseases, terrifying encounters with killer lions and the final disintegration of the marriage to contend with. But husband and wife found common cause in a battle to curb the random slaughter of wild animals. Decades in advance of today's conservation concerns, they embarked on a campaign to persuade local hunting tribes to create the Moremi Wildlife Reserve.

0 552 99426 X

DIANA'S STORY

BY DERIC LONGDEN

'A remarkable book, warm and sad ... laced with a lot of humour'
Sunday Express

In 1971 Deric Longden's wife Diana fell ill with the mysterious disorder known as ME (myalgic encephalomyelitis). She was unable to move without a wheelchair, and was in almost constant pain. Equally distressing, perhaps, was the fact that every doctor she saw was unable to diagnose what was wrong with her. Deric, devoting more and more time to looking after Diana, watched his business gradually fail, and had to neglect his developing career as a broadcaster. He became house husband, nurse and caretaker of the woman he loved.

Diana's Story, far from being one of gloom and despair, is poignant, courageous, and frequently moving. Told by a writer who can transform the bleakest moments with his warmth and wit, it is an extraordinarily funny account of a marriage based on love and on an exceptional sense of humour.

'A funny, sad and, above all, enormously inspiring story'
Clare Francis

0 552 13550 X

LOST FOR WORDS

BY DERIC LONGDEN

'You know, Deric – ten minutes of this rain will do more good in half an hour than a fortnight of ordinary rain would do in a month.'

Deric Longden's mother had a marvellously dotty way with words and a very private brand of logic. She was one of the most amusing and endearing characters in *Diana's Story*, which Deric wrote some years after his wife's Diana's death from what was subsequently believed to be a form of ME. Deric's mother is the central figure in *Lost for Words*, which takes the story forward to the time after Diana's death, and back to his own childhood. Here we find her making her devastating way through Marks & Spencer, conversing with her two cats – almost as eccentric as herself – offering her inimitable comments on the fresh developments in Deric's life, and finally enduring the stroke that led eventually to her death. Sad though the ending is, Deric Longden's gift for blending pathos with rich humour once again offers us far more laughter than tears.

'A lovely read'

Good Housekeeping

0 552 13769 3

A SELECTION OF FINE AUTOBIOGRAPHIES AND BIOGRAPHIES AVAILABLE FROM CORGI AND BLACK SWAN

☐	99065 5	THE PAST IS MYSELF	*Christabel Bielenberg*	£4.99
☐	13582 8	THE GOD SQUAD	*Paddy Doyle*	£4.99
☐	99418 9	A HOME BY THE HOOGHLY	*Eugenie Fraser*	£4.99
☐	12833 3	THE HOUSE BY THE DVINA	*Eugenie Fraser*	£5.99
☐	99425 1	A HOUSE WITH FOUR ROOMS	*Rumer Godden*	£4.99
☐	99347 6	A TIME TO DANCE, NO TIME TO WEEP	*Rumer Godden*	£4.99
☐	13587 9	EVERY LETTER COUNTS	*Susan Hampshire*	£3.99
☐	13586 0	SUSAN'S STORY	*Susan Hampshire*	£2.99
☐	13550 X	DIANA'S STORY	*Deric Longden*	£3.99
☐	13769 3	LOST FOR WORDS	*Deric Longden*	£3.99
☐	99417 0	EDWIN LUTYENS	*Mary Lutyens*	£6.99
☐	13356 6	NOT WITHOUT MY DAUGHTER	*Betty Mahmoody*	£3.99
☐	99463 4	DOROTHY: MEMOIRS OF A NURSE	*Dorothy Moriarty*	£4.99
☐	13732 4	A MOTHER'S WAR	*Fey Von Hassell*	£4.99
☐	99426 X	STARLINGS LAUGHING	*June Vendall Clark*	£5.99
☐	12072 3	KITCHEN IN THE HILLS	*Elizabeth West*	£2.50
☐	11707 2	GARDEN IN THE HILLS	*Elizabeth West*	£2.50
☐	10907 X	HOVEL IN THE HILLS	*Elizabeth West*	£3.50

ORDER FORM